DOING YOUR RESEARCH PROJECT WITH DOCUMENTS

A Step-By-Step Guide to Take You from Start to Finish

Aimee Grant

Foreword by Helen Kara

P

First published in Great Britain in 2022 by

Policy Press, an imprint of
Bristol University Press
University of Bristol
1–9 Old Park Hill
Bristol
BS2 8BB
UK
t: +44 (0)117 954 5940
e: bup-info@bristol.ac.uk

Details of international sales and distribution partners are available at
policy.bristoluniversitypress.co.uk

© Aimee Grant 2022

British Library Cataloguing in Publication Data
A catalogue record for this book is available from the British Library

ISBN 978-1-4473-4403-2 paperback
ISBN 978-1-4473-4404-9 ePub
ISBN 978-1-4473-6394-1 ePdf

Cover design: Nicky Borowiec
Image credit: iStock/Dan Comaniciu
Bristol University Press and Policy Press use environmentally responsible
print partners.
Printed and bound in Great Britain by CMP, Poole

Contents

Detailed contents

List of figures

List of tables

List of boxes

List of sketch notes

List of resources

List of abbreviations

AoIR	Association of Internet Researchers
ASH	Action on Smoking and Health
CAQDAS	Computer Assisted Qualitative Data Analysis Software
DIN	Document Identification Number
ESRC	Economic and Social Research Council
NHS	(UK) National Health Service
NIHR	(UK) National Institute for Health Research
UK	United Kingdom
USA	United States of America

About the author

Aimee Grant is a qualitative researcher with a long-standing interest in developing qualitative methods and research that promote health and equality. She is currently Senior Research Officer at Swansea University's Centre for Lactation, Infant Feeding and Translation (LIFT). Her work focuses on two areas. First, motherhood, health behaviours and stigma, particularly in working-class and Autistic communities. Second, Aimee is involved in evaluating a range of government policies and interventions aiming to improve health. She is the **author** of a collection of six documentary analysis case studies titled *Doing Excellent Social Research with Documents: Practical Examples and Guidance for Qualitative Researchers* (Routledge, 2019). Alongside her research, Aimee has taught a broad range of social science topics at Cardiff University and the University of South Wales, including social research methods, social policy, health and well-being, criminology, and education. She regularly supervises students' dissertation research projects.

Acknowledgements

This book is the product of almost two decades' worth of experience as a student, and then as a researcher and lecturer. So many people have influenced this work. First, Mark Drakeford, my undergraduate dissertation, master's dissertation and PhD supervisor, who encouraged me to use documents as data to explore homelessness, social care and welfare reform. Second, Gareth Williams, who joined my supervisory team for my MSc and PhD and introduced me, a social policist who was scared of **theory**, to medical sociology, including the construction of the patient within medical case files. The Cardiff University **Ethnography** Group, established by Sara Delamont and Paul Atkinson and later chaired by William Housley, has provided a fertile ground for exploring and developing qualitative methods. Likewise, working for Shantini Paranjothy, an epidemiologist, impacted on my methodological clarity and reporting, which I use in this book. I established the Documents Research Network with George Jennings and Maria Pournara, which resulted in rich interdisciplinary discussions between the three of us, and our guest bloggers who drove forward methodology in documentary analysis. I also need to acknowledge the students that I have taught and supervised, who have shaped the way that I communicate research methods and methodology through their questions and our discussions. Likewise, the Women in Academia Support Network (WIASN) has provided support in so many ways, including providing case studies for this book from a broad range of disciplines. My wonderful January Yoga Motivation women – Jen, Karen, Kay, Roberta and Shirin – have been the equivalent of my 'dissertation buddies', keeping me motivated at times when getting this book finished on time *and* good enough felt impossible. Practical help in everyday life, necessitated by my disabilities, has been given by Matt and my wonderful cleaners, Leanne, Mark and Mary, without whom I would not have been well enough to write. A week before submission, the UK Department for Work and Pensions funded a personal assistant for me through the Access to Work scheme (which aims to 'level the playing field for Disabled people in the workplace'). Jasmine Shadrack and Jess Farr-Cox (thefilthycomma.co.uk) stepped in to proofread and did an excellent job in a very short period of time; thank you both. Any remaining mistakes are, of course, mine.

As well as the people, I gratefully acknowledge the funding that has allowed me to undertake the research that has shaped my methodology, and the lessons I will share here. This includes:

- the UK Economic and Social Research Council (ESRC), who funded my MSc and PhD;
- the Welsh Government, who funded my first post-doctoral role at the Cardiff Centre for Journalism, Media and Communication Studies;

- the British Heart Foundation, who funded my post at Action on Smoking and Health (ASH) Wales, which introduced me to the wide range of documentary analysis undertaken to regulate organisations whose products are harmful to human health;
- Public Health Wales NHS Trust, where I undertook research including documentary analysis of meeting agendas and notes to **triangulate** and expand on interview data, to describe how public health interventions work;
- Health and Care Research Wales, who funded my substantive Research Fellow post with Prof Shantini Paranjothy, where I secured funding from a range of organisations to undertake documentary analysis and use visual and creative methods to understand health decision making, including the National Institute for Health Research (NIHR), the Cardiff University Respiratory Bequest Fund, the Wellcome Trust and the ESRC;
- The National Institute for Health Research, who funded my post on a project examining how to reduce child deaths within UK hospital wards using ethnographic methods, including the construction of written patient records and the use of these records by other health professionals;
- Routledge, who commissioned my first book, comprising a series of documentary analysis case studies;
- The Wellcome Trust, who part-funded a Fellowship to examine breastfeeding in public, including an analysis of policy documents;
- finally, Policy Press, who commissioned this book, which encouraged me to really get back to the fundamentals of the method.

Foreword

Helen Kara
Director, We Research It Ltd

The number of documents in the world is both incalculable and increasing at a phenomenal rate. Billions of new books, magazines, leaflets, letters, wills, policies and other documents are created in the world each year. And every day, millions of reports, millions of blog posts, millions of column inches of news media, millions of photos, millions of video transcripts and billions of other documents are published on the internet. Every. Single. Day.

For researchers, this proliferation of potential data wears a Janus face. It evokes both a beautiful dream (all that lovely data!) and a horrible nightmare (will we ever find the data we actually want, and if we do, is there any way to analyse it effectively?). Aimee Grant's book is designed to banish the nightmare and encourage us to realise our dreams.

In this context, it may seem a little ironic that this book explains how to use existing documents to create yet another document. But until humanity invents an alternative to documentation, which my crystal ball does not foresee happening any time soon, no doubt documents will continue to multiply. In which case we researchers might as well make the best of them – and that is exactly what this book can help us to do.

The existence and the quantity of available documents are not the only reasons for using them as data. There are good ethical reasons too. Documents are, in research terms, secondary data: created for some other purpose, then collected and re-used by researchers. People often think of research in association with primary data, because that is the most visible aspect: the person in the street with a clipboard or a tablet, the questionnaire linked in an email or posted through your door. The collection of primary data has become constant and unremitting. Almost every interaction with an organisation leads to a request for feedback, almost every purchase generates a request for a review – and that is before any actual researchers get involved. This leads to 'research fatigue', where potential participants feel disinclined to help because they are tired of responding. There are increasing calls for researchers to try to answer our questions using secondary data first, and only turn to primary data collection when that is really necessary, so as not to overburden potential research participants.

Also, working with documents can improve researchers' wellbeing. Digital or digitised documents can be accessed from anywhere with an internet connection, making them accessible to Disabled researchers, researchers who are carers, researchers who cannot afford to travel and other marginalised researchers. It is often cheaper and quicker to gather documentary data than to gather primary data, which reduces demands on research budgets and timescales. And most electronic documents can be quickly and easily searched for relevant content, which facilitates analysis.

So far, so good: there are lots of documents and good ethical reasons for us to use them in research. But then we start to run into problems. Why should we use documents in our own research? How should we use documents? What are the ethical considerations of doing research with documents? How and where can we find the documents we need? How should we assess their quality? What are the implications of our assessments? How can we analyse our documents? What conclusions can we draw from our work?

These questions, and more, are answered by Aimee Grant. She helps the reader navigate the maze of decisions they need to make, showing how to avoid dead ends and take the shortest path from start to finish. The book is written for students, who will no doubt find it indispensable. I think it would also be useful for early career researchers and researchers outside academia who are new to using documents in their work.

For some years I have been teaching a one-day course on 'documents as data' to postgraduate and early career researchers, based on previous books on the subject. This book is the one I will recommend to my students from now on.

Overview

In the twenty-first century, society is increasingly digital and occurs within virtual spaces. Additionally, there are many benefits of using documents as data (including their ready availability) that make them ideal for dissertation students. This book is a guide on how to undertake your research project using documents, *and* how to write up your dissertation; these are two different skills, and both are necessary to achieve a high grade. The book is structured along the chronological journey of your dissertation project. It starts with advice on working with your supervisor to avoid conflict, project planning, and how to ensure you follow good research practice in relation to **reflexivity, positionality** and ethics. In Part II, the guidance is around reviewing literature, searching for sources, choosing an analysis strategy and writing **research questions**. In this section, you will find a range of questions, templates and to-do lists; these can be slotted into your draft dissertation chapters, making writing up less burdensome. Finally, Part III gives very practical guidance on how to store your data and writing during the research process, assess data quality and write up your dissertation. Within each chapter, you will find case studies from research projects to illustrate methodological points, as well as tips and checklists to keep your dissertation on track.

All the resources included in this book are available to download on the book's website at https://policy.bristoluniversitypress. co.uk/doing-your-research-project-with-documents/online-resources. Look for the Online Resources logo throughout the book.

1

Introduction

Summary

Reading this chapter will help you decide whether you would prefer to use documents as data in your own research or use an alternative data source. The first section of this chapter gives a brief overview of who this book is aimed at before outlining the structure of the three parts of the book: *Getting going*, *Making decisions*, and *Getting it done!* Next, in the main part of the chapter, I provide a brief answer to the question 'what is a document?' I then move on to give brief answers to the questions 'why might we want to do research with documents?' and 'when is it appropriate to do research with documents?' The final section describes why I wrote this book. At the end of the chapter, as in all chapters within this book, you will find a list of further reading; in this case, the chapters and books are focused on documentary analysis in general.

Objectives

By reading this chapter, you should understand:

- what a document is;
- how documents can help us understand society;
- when it is appropriate to use documents in research;
- why I wrote this book.

Is this book for me?

This book is designed to support students who are undertaking dissertation projects which use documents as data, and researchers who are new to documentary analysis. If you are a second- or third-year undergraduate, this book is likely to give you a solid enough grounding in documentary analysis to get you through all stages of your research project. Of course, you are likely to benefit from the use of some additional book chapters or journal articles recommended in each of the chapters of this book, and discipline-specific texts as advised by your supervisor. If you are a master's or doctoral student or a researcher who is new to documentary analysis, I would say that this book is a good starting point. A decent skim of this book will give you a solid knowledge base, and you should then supplement your reading with reference to other core documentary analysis texts, which will be signposted for advanced readers at the end of each chapter.

Structure of the book

In this book, each chapter will take you through the process of doing one part of your research project and will guide you to write notes that will contribute to your dissertation or report. The book is structured chronologically in three parts. First, *Getting going* describes being clear on your research approach, planning your time, maintaining good supervisory relationships, and good scholarship in the form of ethical research and **reflexivity**. These lessons are valuable to you throughout your project. Second, *Making decisions* describes the process of searching for literature, documents and a methodology (analysis strategy and **theory**) and how to combine these into a **research question**. This is rarely a neat and linear process, and you may choose to read the chapters in whichever order feels most suitable for you. Finally, *Getting it done!* focuses on the practicalities of collecting and analysing data – including how to code your data – how to assess data quality and creating a full draft of your dissertation. In each chapter along the way, there are descriptions and case studies of good practice, tips and key questions to ask yourself, warnings, and checklists. The most important points in the book are often accompanied by a handwritten sketch note to help them stand out to you. For users of screen-reading software, image descriptions are embedded as ALT text.

What is a document?

There is no one set definition of what a document is – sorry for the misleading question. As such, the definition of what documentary analysis is has changed over time, from being considered analysis of 'a written text' (Scott, 1990: 12) to much broader definitions in more recent decades (see, for example: Prior, 2003; Grant, 2019). For the sake of being user-friendly, we can call a document:

> A written, graphical, or drawn artefact that is trying to transmit information.

You can see a flow diagram in Figure 1.1 that works through the definition in a step-by-step manner. Let's expand that definition, for the sake of clarity. First, it includes written, drawn or other graphic content; it is not necessary for a document to simply be a plain white page with black writing on it. I chose the word artefact to convey that we aren't necessarily just talking about paper documents, but we can think of advertisements on the side of a bus, signs and even stone carvings. The final element is that, for me, something becomes a

Figure 1.1: Is the thing I'm looking at a document?

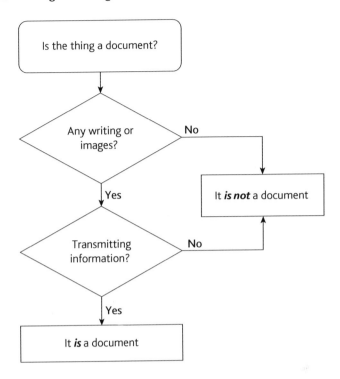

document when it is holding or aiming to share some sort of information or beliefs. So, in this definition, a blank page would not be a document, unless there was context that showed that the blank page was purposefully used to make a point.

The way that we communicate changes over time and, as we use different technology to share the same sorts of information, we should include those new technologies within our definition of documents (Grant, 2019). For example, when I was a child in the 1980s, when I went on holiday, I would send **postcards** to friends and family. These days it might be more normal to share photos and messages on social media, rather than a paper-based medium. These electronic documents, of course, can tell us as much about society as hard paper documents did 50 years ago, and thus are considered documents for the purposes of this book.

If you are still not sure if the data you are considering is a document or not, a second thing to consider is whether somebody, or a group of people, created the content, with the intention that somebody, or multiple people, would consume the document in some way. This can include a careful and detailed reading, or a passing glance. The individual(s) consuming the document can include the author(s), who would return to this document at a later point, for example to help them remember information, such as within a diary or to-do list.

How can documents help us understand society?

A relevant question to consider is 'why might we want to do research with documents?' In this section I will briefly highlight the advantages of using documents as data to understand society. For those considering using documentary analysis, especially postgraduates, a list of additional reading is provided at the end of the chapter.

Advantages to using documents as data

You could definitely say that I have a preference for using documents as data, so this section is likely to be **biased** in favour of documents. My preference is for many reasons, both practical and methodological. In terms of practicalities, as a Disabled academic, I can undertake the research at whatever time suits me best, unlike with other qualitative data–collection methods. Furthermore, when I did not have an academic contract and so could not access a **research ethics committee**, I knew that academic journals would happily publish documentary analysis without **ethical approval**, as the written word is divorced from the spoken word and thus the person. This can, of course, lead to unethical practice, which is discussed in more detail in Chapter 5. Considering methodological reasons, there is such a broad range of written information available in society, much of it now written by ordinary people rather than just the elite, that ignoring it would not allow a rounded understanding of social life. Furthermore, researchers can unobtrusively collect data on almost any subject, although of course there are ethical implications and potential issues in relation to **bias** to consider. I have summarised a list of benefits to using documents as data in Box 1.1.

> ### Box 1.1: Why you might want to do research using documents as data
>
> - Data are often easily accessible, and challenges for data collection can often be foreseen, which is not always the case when trying to identify individuals to take part in interviews, etc. This can be a considerable advantage for those who are Disabled, are working alongside their studies, or have caring responsibilities, as time spent collecting data is often more flexible.
> - Data are generally ready for analysis, without the need for **transcription** or other labour from the researcher.
> - **Sensitive topics** and topics that it might be difficult for you to research (for example, due to your lack of access to a particular group) can be considered from a distance.
> - Using pre-existing data can be viewed as less wasteful than creating new data.

- Documents – including digital content – are increasingly **prevalent** in our society, and it is not possible to understand some aspects of society without including analysis of them.
- A large range of **ontologies** and **epistemologies** can be accommodated within research paradigms used with documents.
- A large number of theoretical approaches can be used within documentary analysis, meaning that it is suitable for a broad range of academic disciplines, from medicine where **theory** is largely absent from research, to sociology where **theory** is strongly embedded throughout research.

When is it appropriate to use documents in research?

Above, I very much focused on the positives of research with documents. However, as with all research strategies, there will be some downsides, both practical and methodological. The main practical downside in my experience is the relative isolation when doing research using documents as data; that is, that you as an individual sit at a desk, quietly searching for or coding data without interacting with another human being. This may result in periods of feeling overwhelmed, bored, or even upset when the data are disturbing. In order to plan ways to protect your mental health in advance of these feelings, please see Chapter 6, which focuses on **reflexivity**.

Considering methodological limitations, there are many that have been proposed, although I believe that many are borne out of a positivistic **epistemology**, which is often considered inappropriate in qualitative research (for more detail about how **epistemology** fits with documentary analysis, see Box 2.2 in Chapter 2). First, we are required to assume **meaning** and intent behind words. Likewise, we cannot ask any follow-up questions of the **author**. While we can use literature and other documents to contextualise the documents under study, and to rationalise our interpretation of **meaning**, this will never be as strong as, for example, a well conducted interview. If **rapport** is developed, an interview-based approach can lead to a wide range of unexpected insights. These insights can be further broadened by using a **visual or creative** methods approach, which asks participants to create a document ahead of an interview and to then describe and elaborate on their document and its **meaning**.

As always, unless your **research question** is very narrow, there will be multiple ways it can be answered; none of these are intrinsically right or wrong, just more or less appropriate methodologically and in terms of practicalities such as time and resources. If you are feeling unsure about whether you should use documents as your dissertation data, I suggest that you read a minimum of one of the chapters in the further reading at the end of this chapter and then discuss your concerns with your supervisor. You may find it helpful to write – and if necessary, take along to your supervision – a list of pros and cons related to your particular topic and potential data sources.

Conclusion: Why I wrote this book and what I hope it will do

As well as reading about why I think this book might be useful for you, I thought you might be interested to know why this book would have been useful for me, had it existed, when I was an undergraduate. As a student, I analysed documents as part of my undergraduate, master's and doctoral dissertations. But I felt as though I was going on 'common sense' advice from my supervisors, more than a robust literature base. I wasn't sure how I could include documents that I had been given, but weren't in the public domain, in my reference list. Now I know that the answer is that they don't go in your reference list if they are data; they go in your methods chapter. It was these small details that it was hard to find an accessible and authoritative text to guide me on.

During my doctoral studies, I read the core documentary analysis books (Scott, 1990; Prior, 2003) recommended at the time – and still recommended by me today – but found it difficult to apply the conceptual lessons in practice. This led me to write a book of case studies of documentary research (Grant, 2019), in order to showcase *how* and *why* I had made decisions in relation to research design at each stage. In writing that book, I realised that I could further distil my knowledge into a very practical step-by-step guide suited to those who were relatively new to documentary analysis. I hope that in doing so, I will help you find making decisions in relation to research design, such as **research questions**, sampling and which analysis strategy to use, much easier than I did when I was beginning my research career. If you read this book and find that I don't do that, please do tell me – I mean it when I say that this is written very much to be helpful to **readers** and if future editions can be improved, that would be great. You can find me on Twitter: @DrAimeeGrant.

Further reading: General sources for documentary analysis
Single chapters in research methods textbooks

Many qualitative research methods textbooks include a single chapter on documentary analysis. These are some of my favourites:

Coffey, A. (2013) 'Analysing documents', in U. Flick (ed) *The SAGE Handbook of Qualitative Data Analysis*, London: SAGE, pp 367–379.

Grant, A. (2020) 'Documents as data: burrowing into the heart of educational institutions', in M. Ward and S. Delamont (eds) *Handbook of Qualitative Research in Education*, Cheltenham: Edward Elgar, pp 299–308.

Largan, C. and Morris, T. (2019) *Qualitative Secondary Research: A Step-by-Step Guide*, London: SAGE, pp 121–143.

Merriam, S.B. (2009) *Qualitative Research: A Guide to Design and Implementation*, San Francisco, CA: Wiley, pp 139–164.

Rapley, T. (2018) *Doing Conversation, Discourse and Document Analysis (Qualitative Research Kit)*, London: SAGE, pp 123–128.

Documentary analysis textbooks

For those of you who are undertaking doctoral research, or who are keen to read more about documentary analysis, the key textbooks are:

Grant, A. (2019) *Doing Excellent Social Research with Documents: Practical Examples and Guidance for Qualitative Researchers*, Abingdon: Routledge.

Largan, C. and Morris, T. (2019) *Qualitative Secondary Research: A Step-by-Step Guide*, London: SAGE.

Plummer, K. (2001) *Documents of Life 2: An Invitation to a Critical Humanism*, London: SAGE.

Prior, L. (2003) *Using Documents in Social Research*, London: SAGE.

Scott, J. (1990) *A Matter of Record: Documentary Sources in Social Research*, London: John Wiley & Sons.

Collections of documentary analysis case studies

If you are feeling that everything you have read so far is too abstract, it may help to consult articles or chapters that report documentary analysis research. These collections by Lindsay Prior and John Scott may not be in your libraries, but you can see the table of contents on the SAGE website; and all of the chapters were previously articles published in journals, which you may find easier to access.

Prior, L. (2011) *Using Documents and Records in Social Research*, London: SAGE.

Scott, J. (2006) *Documentary Research*, London: SAGE.

'How to do a research project' books

These are some of my favourites and should all be accessible to undergraduate students:

Bell, J. and Waters, S. (2014) *Doing Your Research Project: A Guide for First-time Researchers*, New York: Open University Press.

Gardiner, M. and Kearns, H. (2020) *The Seven Secrets of Highly Successful Research Students*, Adelaide: Think Well.

Mason, J. (2018) *Qualitative Researching*, London: SAGE.

Merriam, S.B. (2009) *Qualitative Research: A Guide to Design and Implementation*, San Francisco, CA: Wiley.

O'Leary, Z. (2017) *The Essential Guide to Doing your Research Project*, London: SAGE.

PART I

Getting going

Doing your first big research project can be a steep – sometimes very steep – learning curve. Sometimes you will have excellent support from your supervisor or from peers who are undertaking similar projects. But that is not always the case; supervisors have limited time, and peers may use very different methods, or be too stressed or busy themselves to help you. This may feel frightening, especially if a large part of your degree classification depends on it or it is the first time you have done any research. However, you have the power to really shape what you are researching and learning about, which is pretty exciting.

To make your dissertation feel more exciting and less anxiety-inducing, this part of the book will introduce you to five topics that will help you *throughout* your dissertation. I recommend you read these BEFORE there is a problem. Briefly, the chapters cover: research paradigms and topics; planning and time management; working with your supervisor; ethical issues; and **positionality** and how to be **reflexive**. Below you can read more about the contents of each chapter.

Detailed description of chapters

Chapter 2

Research is not, and in the view of most qualitative researchers can never be, neutral or objective. That is because it is undertaken by humans and involves interpretation. The way that you view documents and understand them to function within society will have an impact on your research. In this chapter, I support you to consider what your **ontology**, **epistemology** and research paradigms are, and how that will impact your research. Also, because it can be overwhelming to even begin to choose a topic when there are *so many* interesting things going on in the world, I will also provide tools to support you to choose a broad topic of interest.

Chapter 3

Your department will issue a dissertation handbook, containing guidance and marking criteria that your examiners use. In this chapter, I guide you through getting the most out of these documents. Following this, I move on to consider ways of planning your time. This has important implications in terms of giving broadly equal time and energy to each of your chapters and so that you still get to do things that are important (and/or necessary) as well as your dissertation. Finally, I acknowledge that many plans are altered due to unforeseen circumstances, so I suggest ways of getting yourself back on track, altering your project if necessary.

Chapter 4

One common issue relating to dissertation students' dissatisfaction is that their supervisor is not supporting them as they believe they should. Frustration and conflict within a relationship with a clear power hierarchy is rarely beneficial to the less powerful individual, in this case the student. In this chapter, I introduce you to the roles of dissertation supervisors, which vary by country, institution and even department. Having contextualised the boundaries of the contemporary student/supervisor relationship, the chapter finally considers how you can identify and implement a suitable working and communication style.

Chapter 5

As a dissertation student – especially using documents as data – research ethics can feel arbitrary and isolated from your lived experience of your research project. When you know that you mean no harm to your research participants, filling in the necessary paperwork to allow your dissertation to begin can feel tedious and sometimes even pointless. This chapter stands back from those forms and considers ethical principles, professional codes and even the reputation of the research community as important forms of researcher integrity. In so doing, it asks you to think about ethics as a big picture element that runs through your entire dissertation. This includes the literature that you choose to review, the questions you choose to ask and whether there are any inherent **biases** in them. In considering a broader definition of ethical research, lazy scholarship can be avoided, and ultimately better research is undertaken.

Chapter 6

Positionality means your impact on the research, and **reflexivity**, or being reflective, is the process of assessing your **positionality**. Ethical practice and **reflexivity** go hand-in-hand; you cannot have one without the other. In this chapter, I provide an overview of **reflexivity** and **positionality** within research, including a rationale for its importance in documentary analysis, including when the **authors** are not involved. Alongside this, I introduce you to practical tools to facilitate your **reflexive** thinking, including interrogating your own thoughts and reactions and regular use of a research diary. The chapter ends by considering the role of self-care within research, which can often contain emotive data, and provides strategies to support yourself and your peers.

2

Working within a research paradigm and choosing a topic

Summary

Within this chapter, I will provide a brief overview of research paradigms, and the **ontologies** and **epistemologies** that come together to create them, including positivism, interpretivism and pragmatism. Following this, I will guide you to consider what those paradigms mean for research with documents. In addition to having a research paradigm, you can choose to use additional **theory** within your research. The interaction between research paradigms and theories will be discussed to enable you to decide what is most suited to your own research project. Finally, I provide some guidance on identifying the broad topic that you would like to study. The chapter closes by signposting a range of resources that consider research paradigm in relation to documents in more detail.

Objectives

By reading this chapter, you should understand:

- what research paradigms are used in qualitative research;
- what research paradigms are used with documents;
- how to identify your own preferred research paradigm;
- how research paradigms and **theory** can be used together;
- what topic you would like to study.

Introduction: A load of 'ologies' you *really* need to consider (a little bit)

We all have ideas about what *our* research paradigm is, but we don't always put this into words, and we can be in danger of assuming that what we think is the correct way of doing things is the *only* way. This is where disciplinary backgrounds, such as sociology, psychology, medicine and geography, are important. In addition to this, you may have heard words that sometimes terrify students (and even experienced researchers), such as **epistemology** and **ontology**. These terms refer to how we understand the construction of knowledge and how it is interpreted in research. Those ideas may seem abstract if you haven't studied any social **theory**, and you may want to skip ahead to a chapter that feels less painful, but try not to be concerned. This chapter aims to give you enough information to have relevant conversations with your supervisor, if applicable, or to help you discount approaches that you feel don't suit you, so that the amount you need to read from other sources is smaller.

Which research paradigms are used in qualitative research?

When we think about research paradigms, what we are really thinking about is the *nature* of the research approach, which is a combination of **ontology** and **epistemology**. In Box 2.1, traditional approaches to research paradigms are described through three layers: **ontology**, **epistemology** and research design. If these approaches do not feel suited to you, Helen Kara (2017) provides a more complete, but still highly accessible, exploration of 'methodologies, approaches and theories', including 'transformative methodologies' (p 46), such as feminist, participatory and decolonising methodologies. These transformative approaches to social research, Kara argues, go beyond considering research as something that is separate to the reality under study, and instead are founded on the basis of a combination of people, facts and phenomenon being a vehicle to facilitate social change.

Box 2.1: Key concepts: the 'ologies' that lead to your research paradigm

Epistemology and **ontology** are core concepts to consider at the very outset of your research project – the extent of your consideration will vary by discipline. When you combine your **ontology** and **epistemology**, you reach your research paradigm, such as **positivist**, **interpretivist** or pragmatist. Each of the three examples goes from the most to the least **positivist**.

Ontology asks: what is reality? Examples of **ontologies** include:

- There is only one reality.
- There are multiple realities.
- Reality is constantly shifting and negotiated between those within that space and time.

Epistemology is concerned with how you can examine, understand or know reality. Examples of **epistemologies** include:

- Reality can be measured *objectively*.
- Reality requires our interpretation to gain knowledge and understanding.
- No one scientific method can be used to measure all of reality.

Research paradigms are the combination of **ontology** and **epistemology**. Examples include:

- Positivism – where one reality is measured objectively.
- Constructivism/interpretivism – where multiple realities are either constructed (constructivism) or interpreted (interpretivism) to understand **meaning**.
- Pragmatism – where shifting and negotiated realities are understood through the most appropriate research tool.

This book is primarily aimed at qualitative approaches, and so the majority of people reading this book will not subscribe to **positivist** views; that is, that there is an objective truth that research can uncover (see Box 2.1). However, that does not mean that you fully subscribe to **interpretivist** paradigms either. Braun and Clarke (2021) describe two core approaches to using qualitative research (both in dissertations and elsewhere):

- 'add qualitative research and stir'; and
- 'qualitative-centric'.

These two approaches are different because of the research paradigm used. When qualitative methods are 'added' to relatively positivistic **research questions**, researchers and disciplines, this affects the processes undertaken. This approach to qualitative research is regularly undertaken in medicine. Within this approach, Braun and Clarke (2021) note that searching for a 'gap' and critiquing existing research is often used to justify doing the research. By contrast, more 'qualitative-centric' approaches justify their presence because reality is constantly shifting and negotiated, and so even studying the same phenomenon is likely to return interesting and novel findings. Depending on your discipline, your examiners (and/or reviewers of journals) may be more inclined towards the 'add qualitative research and stir' approach; this has been my experience publishing within health and medicine.

What approaches are used in research using documents?

Research with documents is undertaken in so many different disciplines, each with their own (often unspoken) understandings about how documents are conceptualised as objects in everyday life as well as within research studies. This links to the research paradigm under study, as can be seen in Table 2.1. Although

Table 2.1: The effect of research paradigm on documentary analysis

Paradigm/methodology	Ontology of documents	Epistemology of documents
Positivism	Documents are an accurate record of reality.	The 'truth' can be found reliably within documents.
Interpretivism	Documents are a record of *one* reality. Other realities can be found in different documents.	We can find interesting and important things about society within documents when we use curiosity to consider **meaning**.
Pragmatism	Documents *may* provide useful information in relation to *one* reality.	Documentary analysis may not be the most suitable, or the only, approach to understand a particular phenomenon.

I have broken down the table into three research paradigms matching those in Box 2.1, this is simplified, and a great number of sub-methodologies exist. Furthermore, regardless of the paradigm utilised in the study itself, published research undertaken in an interpretivistic way can be framed positivistically, for example using numbers and percentages alongside the reporting of quotations, when required by publishers. Having an idea of how best to present your findings (in order to pass your programme of study, or publish your research findings) will inform the approach that you take to your research paradigm.

The way in which documents are conceptualised, both as artefacts in society and as objects that contain knowledge, will impact on the sorts of **research questions** that are asked of documents, and the type of documents that are used to answer those questions. As can be viewed in Table 2.1, both **interpretivist** and pragmatist research designs will require the researcher to undertake interpretation, while positivistic approaches may report on 'the truth' contained within documents as though it is a singular, unquestionable fact. More detailed exploration of critical ontological approaches to research with documents is described in detail throughout Plummer's *Documents of Life 2* (2001: 4). As he notes, rejecting positivism in documentary analysis requires consideration of **theory** to aid in critical reflection on the *contents* and **meaning** within the documents under study:

> [In the humanities; literature and the arts] there is the counter-prevailing trend away from positivism towards realism, rationalism and the theoretical heavens, a view that sees a concern with mere epiphenomena such as life stories as marginal. Such 'data' require well developed theoretical problematics before they may be interpreted; for these critics, the epistemological status of personal documents becomes highly suspect because they cannot embody 'objective truth' and are mere surface scratchings.

How do I identify my own research paradigm?

Lengthy discussions of why one research paradigm has been chosen over another are not usually found within writing on research. This can make the process by which one selects an approach feel confusing and overwhelming for novice researchers. Within some disciplines, the acceptable research paradigms are well understood. For example, within disability studies, it is common to use transformative paradigms to contribute towards societal change. By contrast, **positivist** approaches are relatively common within mainstream medicine and much health research. Within your research methods teaching, if you have been fortunate enough to have some, you may have come to understand the accepted views of knowledge in your discipline. If you feel unsure, speak with your supervisor or refer to some of the further reading at the end of the chapter to help understand your own **ontology**, **epistemology** and research paradigm. This will, in turn, influence any **theory** you use within your study and the analysis approach that you adopt.

There is no wrong approach, as long as you can defend it and carry out your research within its parameters. However, within Plummer's (2001) excellent exploration of critical humanism as a paradigm, you can also see that there may also be no right approach either:

Sketch note 2.1: Don't forget to invite research paradigms to your dissertation

A very specific, narrow, 'westernized' version (of humanism) has simultaneously been made dominant and then been heavily discredited. Indeed, the twentieth century witnessed attacks on 'humanism' from all sides. Behaviourists claimed it was too subjective. Religions – old and new – claimed it was too materialist. Pessimists saw the history of the twentieth century unfolding as evidence of man's accelerating inhumanity to man along with the end of progress thus enshrined. 'Deconstructionists' saw 'man' as a 'fiction' (and a gendered one at that!), claimed the 'death of the author', and reconstructed 'him' as 'subjectivities' found in 'discourse', 'regimes of truth', and 'technologies of the self'. Indeed, with the arrival of the postmodern, 'human beings' and 'humanism' are seen as 'master narratives' whose day is over. All in all, humanism and all it stands for has become a dirty word. (Plummer, 2001: 256)

To ensure you are best placed to be awarded the highest marks possible for this part of your research design, I recommend inserting a paragraph at the least into your methods chapter, unless it is absolutely clear that this is not accepted practice within your department. In Box 2.2, you can find an example of how a student chose their research design and ontology.

Box 2.2: Student example: choosing a research design, epistemology and ontology (Kowalski, 2020: 21–29)

In her MA dissertation on missing people reports in Canada, Larissa Kowalski provides a clear description of her rationale for using a particular research design and **ontology** within her mixed-methods research. She notes that she chose a convergent parallel design because it allowed:

• equal weight to be given to qualitative and quantitative data;
• reporting of the qualitative and quantitative data separately;
• differences between the data sources to be considered.

This was important, she notes, because of the tensions between the qualitative and quantitative data. Kowalski goes on to note that although a pragmatist in terms of **ontology**, the debates within pragmatism meant that the **ontology** didn't feel quite right for her in this project. Instead, she identified more with dialectical pluralism 'because I explicitly sought a "synergistic benefit" from integrating both post-positivist and interpretivist paradigms' (p 26).

What is the difference between research paradigm and theory?

Once you have a clear idea of your research paradigm, you may be thinking that you have made the big decisions. However, alongside your research paradigm, which is focused on how knowledge is constructed, a range of theoretical perspectives can be used. Grand theories are made based on observations of how a society, or societies, function. For example, Marxist **theory** focuses on how society is shaped by capitalism, and how social class is maintained to the detriment of the working class, in order to maintain income inequality.

Alongside grand theories, mid-range theories tend to be focused on a narrower and more specific part of society or may be based on psychological understandings of thought and behaviour. There are so many mid-range theories that it is not possible to provide an overview of them, but some examples can be found in Table 2.2. When reading around the topic area that you are considering investigating, you may find it beneficial to make notes regarding which **theory** was adopted and – if stated – why, within individual studies.

Why should I use theory in my research?

Once you have established an appropriate **theory**, or even multiple theories, that relate to your research topic and question, the **theory** can become part of the structure of your analysis. For example, if a feminist approach is adopted, the analysis will be focused on gender, and gender inequality. At times, the use of one single **theory** may feel inadequate, and here it is possible to use more than one **theory** to frame your research project. Alternatively, you may be able to find a mid-range **theory** combining elements from a range of theoretical perspectives that is best suited to the phenomena under study. Box 2.3 highlights the use of **theory** in a master's thesis based on records collected in libraries.

Table 2.2: Mid-range theories

Name (core reference)	Overview	Discipline
Street-level Bureaucracy (Lipsky, 2011)	Considers how publicly funded organisations deliver services in an environment where there is more demand than resources.	Social policy
Critical Autism Studies (Woods et al, 2018)	Rejects ableist approaches to the study of Autism, foregrounding the humanity of Autistic people and the value of different neuro types.	Health
Actor Network Theory (Latour, 2005)	Objects in the environment, as well as human and non-human sentient beings, are 'actors'. All actors contribute to behaviour.	Science and technology studies
Capability, Opportunity, Motivation – Behaviour (COM-B) (Michie et al, 2011)	Individuals' behaviours are explained, and determined, by their capability, opportunity and motivation for engaging in an individual behaviour.	Psychology

Sketch note 2.2: Theory adds depth and sparkle to your research

Box 2.3: Student example: using theory within an analysis of library administrative records (Skinner, 2015)

Within Julia Skinner's (2015) doctoral dissertation, she considered library administrative records, situated in a research paradigm that appears to be **interpretivist**, positioning her form of documentary analysis as qualitative **content analysis**. The data included board meeting minutes, annual reports, letters and other records (p 51). Within the analysis, Skinner notes the importance of what *is not* said, alongside what is recorded; for example, heated debates being omitted from the official records. Skinner uses this information as context to frame her analysis, but it is also formally included in the analysis through the use of the information worlds **theory**. Information worlds **theory** positions documents as interwoven with their surroundings, which has an impact on how information is recorded, shared and conceptualised within individual 'worlds'.

How do I choose a research topic?

This question has no simple answer. Sometimes, you will be given free rein to pick any topic that is within your degree. Other times, supervisors post lists of topics that you have to choose between. Somewhere in the middle lie departments where you are expected to find a supervisor, who may then have ideas for topics that you can mould to your interests. When you have an element of freedom, it can feel overwhelming. Petra Boynton (2016) suggests that students spend time considering what research skills and interests they have and thinking about the training and support they would need to use particular research methods.

One overwhelming factor is that you should not go into your dissertation hating the topic or finding it boring, dull or uninspiring. Instead, you should have at least a mild level of interest or enthusiasm for the research topic. From this point, you will move on to consider the literature (Chapter 7), data available (Chapter 8) and the sorts of analysis techniques you are interested in using (Chapter 9) before pinning down a final topic and a **research question** (Chapter 10). It may feel a very long way through the book, but that is because it is helpful to know your research topic early in the dissertation process. You may not know your final **research question** until you have done a large volume of preliminary enquiry into your topic. To help you understand how other students chose their dissertation topic, I have minimally altered quotations from sources that are freely accessible online. This approach protects the **authors' anonymity** while allowing you to experience authentic student views.

Sketch note 2.3: Write down your bright ideas

Box 2.4: Students' views on how to choose a research topic

- When I entered my PhD, I was thinking of researching (topic 1). But then I did some checking and that wouldn't be considered valuable to society, as things are changing in how we use (that technology). Instead, I considered (topic 2), but in my opinion it's just another short-lived interest that won't matter in the long term. I settled on (topic 3) within (specific group of people A). This was perfect because it mixed my interest in topic 3, specific group of people A, and my interest in (a sub-area of topic 3). Reflecting on it, I'm surprised my topic and group of people didn't come to me straight away.
- I wanted to do my dissertation on (topic 1), because it really interested me, but it was very difficult to collect the data I needed to, and required costly trips to archives, including one that closed down. My supervisor was pushing me to look into (topic 2) instead, but I didn't want to, because I didn't find it interesting, even though the data would be easy to collect. I stuck with the first topic for a while, but realised I was running out of time. I reluctantly started working on (topic 2). I didn't enjoy it as much, but I passed my dissertation!
- I really enjoyed my lectures with Prof X. I knew that I wanted to do my dissertation with him as it gave me the best option of studying something related to my dream job. So I stayed behind after class and asked if he would consider being my supervisor and asked what topics he was interested in supervising. The first thing he suggested was SO boring, but I liked the idea of (topic 2) and (topic 3) that he suggested. I went away and read up on them and decided that out of the two ideas, I liked (topic 2) better. One of my friends ended up doing (topic 1) with him as her supervisor and really enjoyed it.
- I identified my dissertation topic by looking at every essay I had written during my degree and thinking about what the overarching topic was behind all of the essays I had enjoyed writing. That was how I got to my topic of interest, and it made sure I didn't find out part way through that what I was studying was really boring.

Conclusion

This chapter has provided an overview of **ontology**, **epistemology** and research design in relation to research with documents. As has been shown, a particular set of documents could be considered within multiple different approaches. Alongside considering research paradigm, we have briefly touched on introducing **theory** into your research project, through the use of grand theories and mid-range theories. It can be hard to choose a particular approach, and discussing your thoughts with your supervisor or peers may be beneficial to helping you achieve clarity.

Further reading

Undergraduate

Braun, V. and Clarke, V. (2021) 'Tips on writing a qualitative dissertation or thesis, from Braun & Clarke – Part 1', *Edpsy UK*. Available at: https://edpsy. org.uk/blog/2021/tips-on-writing-a-qualitative-dissertation-or-thesis-from-braun-clarke-part-1/

Kara, H. (2017) *Research and Evaluation for Busy Students and Practitioners*, Bristol: Policy Press. Chapter 3: Methodologies, approaches and theories, pp 41–60.

Postgraduate

Plummer, K. (2001) *Documents of Life 2: An Invitation to a Critical Humanism*, London: SAGE.

Prior, L. (2003) *Using Documents in Social Research*, London: SAGE.

Scott, J. (1990) *A Matter of Record: Documentary Sources in Social Research*, London: John Wiley & Sons.

3

Working productively

Summary

In this chapter, I will take you through different ways of planning and time-management techniques. The first section discusses using the resources available from your university to understand what makes a good dissertation *in your department*; remember, guidance varies considerably by discipline and institution. I will then provide guidance and resources to enable you to make a plan in a format that suits you. The chapter closes by considering what to do if you are not able to keep to your plan, which happens very frequently.

Objectives

By reading this chapter, you should understand:

- what information you need to consult and follow;
- where you are in the research process, and what the next steps are;
- how to make a plan to complete your dissertation in the time you have available;
- what to do if your project doesn't go to plan.

Introduction: Back it up!

Throughout the book you will find the suggestion to back up your research and writing; I would hate for you to lose your work. Before you begin searching for the information you need in order to get a high grade, I suggest setting up an electronic folder where you can save all the information.

Box 3.1 provides a potential filing structure for your research project that you may find helpful to use or modify. It is important that the structure makes sense to you, and helps to avoid wasted time searching for things you have already found, or duplicating effort in other ways.

Sketch note 3.1: Back up your work

Box 3.1: A potential filing structure for your research project

- Dissertation handbook and course guidance
- Reading
  - Background information
  - Literature
  - Methods literature
- Notes
- References
- Ethics and ethical approval
- Data
- Analysis
- Draft chapters
- Feedback from supervisor
- Final version of chapters
- Final dissertation

How can I focus on my dissertation?

Before we think about how to work productively, it may be helpful to think about barriers to productive working. These can be completely overwhelming for students, as one anonymous student writing about their experience of being caught out for plagiarism noted:

Table 3.1: Barriers to focusing on dissertation, from students in the USA

Barrier	Definition/example
Perfectionism	'High performance standards and high self-criticism, leading to increased stress and procrastination and decreased academic achievement' (p 66)
Competing priorities	Family, employment, etc.
Time and project management skills	Particularly related to writing, managing a research project of the size of the dissertation, understanding how long it takes to perform research-related tasks
Writing anxiety	Negatively interacts with student's belief they can complete their dissertation. Originates from fear of failure, hesitancy to begin writing, not completing writing tasks, and chronic procrastination
Challenges with supervisors	Disjointed communication styles and priorities between supervisors and students
Cognitive habits	'All or nothing thinking' and 'jumping to conclusions' (p 67) in relation to feedback on written work can have a negative impact on student's thinking about their dissertation
Individual stressors	Life events separate to the dissertation process

Source: Russell-Pinson and Harris, 2019: 66–68

'[My dissertation] just felt too big, too nebulous. I had no idea where to start. I kept putting it off and putting it off again, with no idea of what to do. I could have asked for help, but I didn't. How pathetic, I thought – every other student can manage to write one, but you need help? Just fucking put your head down and do it. But I didn't.'

Table 3.1 highlights known stressors that can lead to students undertaking a lot of time working (or procrastinating) for limited reward. In many instances, this is not because the student is *bad* or *lazy*, as they may themselves report, but often stems from anxiety and self-criticism. You may find it helpful to think about if you identify with any of these barriers, and if so, consider how you can work towards finding resolutions to help you feel less overwhelmed by your dissertation.

What information should I consult and follow?

Every university, and often each individual school or department within that university, will produce a module handbook. These handbooks contain guidance on how to write a high-quality dissertation and any important dates, such as for submitting proposed projects, ethical approval applications and the final dissertation. This guidance is likely to be found on your department's intranet or within an online learning portal for students who are doing a dissertation in your department. You cannot rely on the procedure being the same across different departments in your university, so it is essential to follow the guidance for your course.

One key element of getting going is finding or being allocated a supervisor. The mechanism to do this will generally be found in your module handbook. If

Sketch note 3.2: Don't panic: plan!

you are responsible for finding a supervisor, try to get in early with the supervisor of your choice: if you think they're likely to be good, lots of other students are also likely to have the same idea. When you approach the supervisor of your choice, you need to ensure that you can tell them *why* you particularly want them to supervise your dissertation (i.e. show enthusiasm for the topic or methods involved). If you are contacting them by email, it is very important to stand out by being interested and polite. There are more tips in the next chapter regarding successful communication with supervisors.

A second core process that will be outlined in your dissertation handbook is the procedure relating to **ethical approval**. It may or may not be clear whether ethical approval is required for a study using documents, so you may need to look on the intranet for further details of the ethics committee who review undergraduate dissertations. University ethics committees often meet once a month, with the deadline to submit application forms sometimes two weeks before the meeting. They are likely to have particular requirements, such as completing a particular form, but also including other documents to go alongside it, such as a rationale for the research (which can be an early draft of your literature review) and any information sheets or consent forms you plan to use to access documents. In some months, such as around religious holidays, there may not be an ethics committee meeting at all that month, due to large numbers of staff being on leave. It is important to find out early on what the procedure is, so you can plan around these deadlines.

Sketch note 3.3: Read the information

Moving on to think about the dissertation itself, there is likely to be guidance directed at students; a marking scheme for your examiners is often also included. Reviewing the marking matrix and thinking like an examiner enables you to consider what needs to be achieved to secure a high grade. Often marking schemes will be broken down into the individual parts of your dissertation, describing what makes a literature review (for example) third-class. This might include the number of items reviewed, but also the sophistication of the linking of different pieces of literature. Resource 3.1 is a checklist of the above information, to facilitate getting the most benefit from the information provided by your department. All the resources included in this book are available to download on the book's website (see the Overview for the link), allowing you to add to or amend them as is most useful to you.

Sketch note 3.4: Think like an examiner

Where am I in the research process? What are the next steps?

This section of the chapter is small but very important, so it gets its own heading. First, I describe a chronological journey through a dissertation in terms of the written report. Throughout the book, in the chapters relevant to

Resource 3.1: Getting the most out of your dissertation handbook

Task	Sub-task	Complete	Notes
Step 1 **Find information**	Dissertation handbook		
	Marking criteria		
	Dissertation learning portal		
	Other		
Step 2 **Extract process info**	What structure and content is expected?		
	Are there any interim deadlines?		
	Final deadline date?		
	Reasons for extenuating circumstances?		
	Other		
Step 3 **Extract ethics info**	Will you need ethical approval? If Yes:		
	-What information do you need to submit?		
	-When do you need to submit?		
	-How long does it take for your project to be reviewed?		
	Other		
Step 4 **Extract marking info**	Review marking criteria:		
	-Differences between grades		
	-Specific points for each chapter		
	-Specific research skills expected		
	Other		

them, more detailed checklists are provided in relation to the literature review (Chapter 7), methods chapter (Chapter 10), results chapter (Chapter 11) and discussion chapter (Chapter 12). In Chapter 13, I describe merging the draft chapters you have written, to create your final dissertation. Second, I consider what to do when you think you've made a big mistake; my key message is don't panic!

The order of the dissertation process and write-up

Often, doing research is presented as a logical, chronological process that you follow from step A to B to C to D. However, the stages of planning your research which occur *before* you start taking steps A, B, C and D involve a lot of flexibility in terms of order. This is when you search for relevant background information, such as policy documents, literature and data sources that will enable you to form a coherent project. It is essential to get to this point where everything aligns, but it does not magically happen and requires curiosity and thinking time from the researcher. Getting things right during the planning stage (Part II of this book), makes doing the research itself (Part III) much easier.

You may be reading this book before starting your project; if so, that is marvellous. Continue reading in roughly chronological order if that works for you. However, I imagine that most **readers** will be coming to this book part way through their dissertations. If you have already completed parts of your research, but have not started to write, you will still benefit from looking at the chapters relating to those areas, to get hints and tips on what to include in each chapter.

If you are writing up a standard research project, your sections or chapters are likely to be arranged something like:

- abstract
- background/introduction
- literature review
- methods
- results
- discussion
- conclusion

These headings are not fixed and, in some disciplines, things will be combined or different names will be used. I suggest that you consult your dissertation handbook or speak to your supervisor (if it is not clear in your handbook), so that you can be clear on the structure that you need to use and ensure that your efforts are directed to the most beneficial place. Something that can help as you are progressing through your dissertation is to have a clear idea of the word count overall and how many words you wish to 'spend' on each chapter. I suggest aiming for a balance, with no chapter too much longer than the others, with the exception of the shorter introduction and conclusions chapters. This allows you to meet the marking criteria relating to each chapter. In Resource 3.2, I provide a template to visualise the structure of a typical dissertation, including possible sub-sections to include in each chapter, along with space for the word count. You may choose to use or amend this resource in your own planning.

Help! I made a really big mistake

Sometimes, part way through a study, you may realise that, for example, your analysis strategy was not the best strategy available to answer your **research question**. The point at which you have this thought is crucial in deciding what you do about it. If you haven't started your analysis yet, I would try out the two different options – the current plan and the other option – on a portion of your data so you can consider the matter (discussing it with your supervisor if possible). However, if you have analysed most of your data and have little time remaining before the deadline, you would usually be best placed to continue as you are. One way to manage this is to include a comment in the strengths and weaknesses part of your discussion that other ways of answering your **research question** are available and would have potentially provided different results. More information on writing about your study's strengths and weaknesses is included in Chapter 12.

How can I make a plan to complete my dissertation in the time available?

In this section, we will look at combining the information you found in the previous section and thinking about how to make a plan that suits you best. First, you will be asked to think about your preferred working style. We will then look at what success means to you. For instance, do you want the best grade possible, or is it important to fit your dissertation into a limited amount of time due to other commitments? I will then take you through ways of displaying plans, and what you might need to fit into your plan (besides your dissertation). As always, the things I'm sharing are my tips, and what suits me may well not suit everybody, so you are always welcome to use whichever method works best for you. We discuss this in more detail in the next section.

An important note about learning and working styles

I am conscious that I am writing this chapter from my own perspective. That is, someone who is incredibly organised as a way of mitigating the memory and executive function issues that are part of being Dyslexic. From my experiences as a supervisor, manager and colleague, however, I know that many researchers do not work using the 'little and often' approach that I take towards research and will do their research in a concentrated burst close to the deadline. Working this way

Resource 3.2: Structuring your dissertation

Chapter	Sub-heading	Word count and %	Notes
Introduction	Introduction to dissertation		
	Why subject is important		
	Relevant changes to society		
	Conclusion & sign post to literature		
Literature review	Introduction to literature review		
	Logically structure your review into sections		
	Conclusion & sign post to methods		
Methods	Introduction (summary of methods) & research question		
	Population and sample		
	Data collection		
	Data analysis strategy		
	Conclusion & sign posting to results		
Results	Introduction (summary of results)		
	Logical presentation of your findings by theme/topic, etc.		
	Conclusion & sign posting discussion		
Discussion/ Conclusion	Introduction (summary of discussion)		
	Summary of results		
	Compare results to literature		
	Strengths and weaknesses		
	Implications for policy/practice		
	Conclusion to entire dissertation		
Finishing touches	Abstract		
	Front matter & appendices		
	Proofreading		

Sketch note 3.5: Do some writing today

would give me so much anxiety that I could not perform at my best, but other people perform their best work under the pressure of an impending deadline.

If you are someone who completes the vast majority of your work close to the deadline, and you anticipate receiving feedback on draft chapters of your work, I suggest an early conversation with your supervisor so that they are clear that this is the way that you intend to work. This prevents misunderstanding and disappointment on both sides. For example, your supervisor may request a copy of your literature review after four weeks. When it is not delivered, the slot that they have saved in their diary in which to read and comment on your literature review is absorbed by something else. When it is given in with other chapters a month later, the supervisor does not have the same amount of time available for each chapter, and so the student's feedback may be less detailed than that received by their peers because of the supervisor's need to rush. By agreeing a rough schedule of chapter deadlines early on, life is made easier for both student and supervisor. That is not to say that your supervisor *will* have time available, but you will be forewarned and able to amend your expectations and plans accordingly.

What does success look like for you?

It is easy for people, including your parents and supervisors, to assume that success for you is achieving the highest mark possible. That may well be true for many people reading this book, because you are the people who made the effort to get the book out of the library or download it and then actually read it. However, your definition of success might be quite different. For example, you may need or wish to juggle multiple commitments alongside your dissertation. When you see your supervisors and other members of teaching staff, they may give an impression of being wholly dedicated to their research. Some academics are like this, but many have more balanced lives, or at least attempt to have balance in their lives. Box 3.2 provides some pointers to help you think about how you can fit your dissertation around existing commitments.

Box 3.2: Fitting your dissertation in

1. Decide how you would like to display your time: a paper diary, electronic calendar or something that you design yourself.
2. Map your existing commitments. Block out time including for things that you:
   a. 'have to do' within university, such as lectures, other teaching, completing assessments and revision;
   b. 'have to do' outside of university, including paid or volunteering work and caring responsibilities;
   c. 'want to do', such as socialising, sports, not working in the evenings or at weekends.
3. Map the project deadlines, including:
   a. supervisor assignments (such as submitting draft chapters);
   b. ethical approval;
   c. the final deadline.
4. Draft in the time you have available for working on your dissertation in blocks of at least 45 minutes.
5. Does it look like you have enough time? If not, consider where you can take some time:
   a. Can you reduce any of the tasks that you have to do outside of university, even if only for a few weeks around the time of your submission?
   b. If you can't find any more time, how are you going to make your project manageable in the time you have? (The answer here is about making it take less time!)

Ways of drawing up plans

There is no definitive agreed way of displaying how to plan your time. The most important thing is that it is easily understandable to you. I will present two methods that I find work well *together*: **Gantt chart**s and to-do lists.

Gantt charts

I am a big fan of the visual representation of multiple things that is achieved within **Gantt chart**s. To make a **Gantt chart**, you create a table, with the dates along the top – usually in months, but perhaps in weeks if you don't have much time, or quarters if you have a lot of time – and the tasks down the left-hand side, with one row per task. The individual boxes get shaded to highlight when the task should be worked on. Resource 3.3 is a **Gantt chart** template over nine periods of time; a blank copy is available online for you to amend and use as is most helpful. I have completed Resource 3.3 as an example, working on the assumption that I had four months to undertake my dissertation, and thus shaded

Resource 3.3: Planning your dissertation using a Gantt chart

Task ➡ Time	Month 1	Month 2	Month 3	Month 4	Month 5	Month 6	Month 7	Month 8	Month 9
Find a supervisor	▓								
Review guidance	▓								
Begin keeping a research diary	▓								
Read literature	▓								
Read ethics literature	▓								
Investigate sources	▓								
Draft literature review									
Read methods literature									
Select analysis method		▓							
Identify sample		▓							
Ethics application									
Draft methods chapter		▓	▓						
Collect data			▓						
Analyse data			▓						
Consider data quality			▓						
Draft results chapter			▓						
Compare results to literature				▓					
Draft discussion chapter				▓					
Update lit. review if required				▓					
Draft abstract				▓					
Incorporate supervisor feedback	▓	▓	▓	▓					
SUBMIT				YIPPEE!!					

out months 5–9. I then tried to plan my tasks in four roughly equal amounts. Looking at this chart, you can see that each month contains a lot of work. If you only have four months, you might find it more useful to break your **Gantt chart** down into 16 weeks, so that you can plan your time more easily and each month looks less overwhelming.

In my example **Gantt chart**, you can see that I did not have enough time to allow any breathing room, in the form of a few spare weeks at the end. However, it is good practice, if you possibly can, to insert at least some contingency time at the end. Challenges to your timeline often occur, in terms of doing your research, but also in family life, including things like whether to go to a festival or on holiday at short notice when you have a large project to complete.

During projects, including writing this book, to keep myself accountable, I print a copy of my **Gantt chart**, and stick it to the noticeboard beside my desk. This means that I can easily check my progress at regular intervals and see if I am starting to slip behind.

To-do lists

To-do lists can be used in so many ways, including breaking down a bigger task. For example, in the **Gantt chart**, 'collect data' is listed, but that is not one single task. It can involve multiple databases, cataloguing the data you have collected and storing it in a logical and accessible manner. It may take several weeks to get through this one task on a **Gantt chart**. Not being able to 'tick off' a job for several weeks could be disheartening; breaking down each task allows you to have regular small victories. Resource 3.4 is an example of a to-do list for a dissertation student who is at an early stage in their project. As well as listing the activity or 'thing' to be done, it provides space for you to add a priority to the task. I tend to use a system of 1–5, with 1 being the most important or urgent task, but you can choose whatever works best for you.

As well as paper-based to-do lists, it is possible to use a broad range of applications (apps) to store (and tick off) your to-do lists. At the time of writing, I am using Trello, which allows me to have a 'board' per project, then ways of dividing even further within the board, including checklists. I have a 'board' for writing, and within that board a 'card' for this book, and within that a 'list' for each chapter. Within each list you can include information, links, PDFs and checklists. I find being able to break things down and access the lists on my phone and computer makes me feel in control of the amount of work I have to do. It also stops me writing too many lists on post-it notes and then losing them or wondering if I made a note to do X when I am away from the office. That's not to say that I don't often end up with paper to-do lists as well, because something that is physically present on my desk is harder to forget than going into an app on my phone. However, these tend to be for the things I need to access most frequently, such as my style guide for this book, which has lived on a sticky note at the base of my monitor for months reminding me that Heading 5 is for figures, Heading

Resource 3.4: Super important dissertation things to do

Priority	Thing	Date needed	Notes
1	Write draft introduction chapter for review by supervisor	End of November	Aim to do by 14th before holiday
1	Read up on topic for intro chapter: media, social media, politicians, grey literature	Aim end of September	Didn't Kim Kardashian insta about it?
3	Find a proofreader for final dissertation	End of April	Asked Angela – waiting for reply
2	Watch BBC Panorama episode on topic	End of October	
1	Find notes from 2nd year module on topic – re-read papers on reading list.	End of September	
2	Draft an email for supervisor to review to help get access to data	Next supervision – October 30th 2pm	

Sketch note 3.6: To-do lists can help you to plan

6 for Boxes, etc. I have another to remind me of the referencing requirements, to stop me using full stops where the Policy Press style guide (my equivalent of the dissertation handbook) tells me to use commas.

What if I feel that my project isn't going well?

In this section, I describe how changes from your plan are very normal within research and how to operationalise changes. Alongside this, I describe how many dissertation students feel overwhelmed and anxious about *doing it wrong*. This is incredibly common, and often unfounded; I'm very sorry if you are feeling this way. Below, I briefly discuss feeling overwhelmed, returning to it more comprehensively within the self-care section of Chapter 6.

The myth of easy order in research

I was once told by a manager (repeatedly!) that 'plans are made to be broken'. This is the case with most research and writing plans, and by the end of the project, if you have printed out your **Gantt chart** it is highly likely that there will be crossings out, extended sections where research tasks or writing takes longer than planned and other assorted annotations. This is not problematic: the plan or **Gantt chart** is an aid to help you realise how much work needs to be done in the time available, not something that you are absolutely held to. It can be used during supervision meetings to highlight the need to catch up or change

Sketch note 3.7: Be aware of key dates

plans, to ensure high-quality work is produced in the remaining time. The key thing to remember is that you need to be finished in time to meet your deadline.

How to change your plan

The way to change your plan is actually very simple; although it's often painful, because of a sense that you have 'gone wrong' by not sticking to the first plan. First, make a list of the tasks left to do. Second, look at the time you have available. Third, combine these. You will likely have to reduce your ideal level of quantity or quality to complete the dissertation on time. If you feel bad about reducing the scope of your plan, it is likely that the original scope was too large to fit within the confines of the dissertation; this is hard to see when you have not previously undertaken similarly complex research projects, so try not to be too hard on yourself.

Help! I feel overwhelmed

It can be very frustrating and overwhelming when your plans are derailed. Now is the time to speak to your peers, family and supervisor. If you feel that they are not able to adequately help you, most universities have student support services, where you can – in theory – access counselling. Within many neoliberal universities, however, counselling services have been cut and may only be available for students who are diagnosed with serious mental ill health. There are many charities that can provide a listening ear if you are in crisis; the Wikipedia 'List of suicide crisis lines'[1] page listed organisations for mental health crisis by country at the time of writing. Please do not suffer alone if anxiety is making you feel unwell.

Conclusion

In this chapter, I showed you a process of looking at the guidance for dissertation students in your department and the marking criteria that your examiners will use. Next, I encouraged you to think about what you have already achieved in relation to your dissertation, and what the next steps are. Once you are clear on what tasks are left to undertake, I described a range of ways to make a plan. These plans are very important to help make sure you don't spend too long on one part of the research process at the expense of other parts, as this can negatively affect your grade. Finally, because life often gets in the way of a good plan, and conducting research can take as much time as you allow, I provided ideas for how to redesign your research project and writing plan if you encounter any of these challenges. Finally, I urged anybody who is feeling unwell because of stress and anxiety to seek support.

Further reading

Undergraduate

Badiru, A.B., Rusnock, C.F. and Valencia, V.V. (2016) *Project Management for Research: A Guide for Graduate Students*, CRC Press: London, pp 75–86.

Levin, P. (2005) *Excellent Dissertations!* Milton Keynes: Open University Press. Part One: Preliminaries, pp 6–23.

Postgraduate

Boynton, P. (2020) 'The research companion blog', *The Research Companion* [online]. Available at: https://theresearchcompanion.com/Blog/ [Accessed 14 January 2021].

Flocke, L.F., Spirduso, W.W. and Silverman, S.J. (2007) *Proposals That Work: A Guide for Planning Dissertations and Grant Proposals*, London: SAGE.

Gardiner, M. and Kearns, H. (2020) 'PhD toolkit', *Think Well* [online]. Available at: www.ithinkwell.com.au/resources/PhDToolkit [Accessed 14 January 2021].

4

Working with your supervisor

Summary

If I had to name the number one issue that students have informally sought me out to discuss, it is definitely challenges with supervisory relationships. This chapter will outline the neoliberal education context that you are likely to be in, and some of the roles that supervisors undertake, although this varies internationally. I also provide an overview of research showing students' and supervisors' thoughts on the supervision process. This knowledge is then used to consider *how* to improve your working relationship with your supervisor, including communication skills.

Objectives

By reading this chapter, you should understand:

- what a supervisor's role is;
- where tension exists within supervisory relationships;
- how to communicate with your supervisor.

Introduction: Sometimes supervisory relationships really suck

Towards the beginning of your final year of study, if you are undertaking a dissertation, you will be allocated a supervisor. The allocation of supervisors varies between countries, institutions and even departments within institutions. In some instances, students will be expected to take the initiative and identify potential supervisors themselves. In other institutions, a list of supervisors and topics will be advertised, and students will be asked to choose from this list, not necessarily being allocated their first choice. This process may feel awkward and uncertain, in comparison to the way in which you have been able to select modules throughout your degree. In my experience, it is relatively rare for undergraduate dissertation students to change supervisors part way through the dissertation period, as it is relatively short. What this means in practice is that students have little opportunity to do anything other than make the situation work as best as

Box 4.1: Higher Education policy and overwork: a pandemic

It is not possible to understand the ways in which supervisors operate without understanding the system that they are working within. In the 1970s, many global North countries with right-wing (conservative) governments moved towards Higher Education policies favouring marketisation, and later neoliberalisation. This meant budget cuts, increased workloads for staff, stress, burnout and even suicide. Alongside this, casual or 'zero hours contracts' staff were used in 46 per cent of UK universities at the time of writing (UCU, 2020), and pensions were set to be devalued, resulting in widespread strikes across the UK from 2017, supported by many students. To make the 'product' (your degree) look high-quality, universities focus on building new teaching and research spaces as an outward show of success and power. This is at the expense of the staff who deliver education. Ultimately, neither university staff nor students benefit from this arrangement.

they can. This is not always easy and may feel uncomfortable. Sometimes it feels unfair. And that absolutely sucks. In dissertations that take place over a longer period, such as master's and doctoral projects, changing supervisors is more likely to occur if a formal complaint is made.

Students sometimes think that they have done something wrong or are disliked by their supervisor when their supervisor is not supportive. Often, however, it is that the supervisor is overloaded with work, or sometimes they just don't prioritise students and teaching commitments above research, which is given more prestige by many universities. Knowing it isn't personal might make things feel easier if you have a difficult working relationship with your supervisor. Box 4.1 provides some context on Higher Education policy, budget cuts and overwork that may contextualise your supervisor's behaviour. That doesn't excuse it and if you are receiving less supervisory support than you are supposed to receive, it isn't OK.

What is my supervisor's role?

In this section, we will consider what is and isn't a supervisor's responsibility in relation to supporting dissertation students. Rather unhelpfully for students, there is no fixed definition of what supervision is or what the supervisory relationship should look like. This can make it difficult to compare the supervision that you are receiving with other students' experiences. That is not to say that one method is intrinsically better than another, but simply to note that supervisors are human, and accordingly we all behave slightly differently, even when following the same guidance. Below, I work through the core roles of a supervisor: performing supervisory meetings; providing advice and guidance; facilitating your skills development; and providing feedback on your progress. These will be used to varying extents within your department. Furthermore, the number of hours that your supervisor is allocated to supervise your work can vary significantly and is often surprisingly low (less than ten hours, including reviewing and marking written work).

Performing supervision, usually through meetings

Supervisory meetings may be face-to-face, by video call or occasionally by telephone. Within these meetings, there is no established structure, but your department may have guidance, either within your dissertation handbook, or on the intranet. Sometimes, a template document is provided in which students can record a summary of the agreed course of actions, and any agreed objectives for themselves and their supervisor. If these template documents are provided, they may be required or optional and it is up to you to investigate the procedure in your department. If you are unable to find a template document and feel that your supervision meetings are not going as well as you would like, you may benefit from using or amending the template meeting pro forma supplied later in this chapter (Resource 4.2).

The number of meetings that you will have can vary dramatically; for example, some undergraduate and even master's programmes may only require you to meet with your supervisor once, in order to gain approval for your project, and then leave you to fend for yourself. Even some doctoral students may simply be left to 'get on with it', as one of the students in my PhD cohort was told by their supervisor, an eminent professor.

Advice and guidance

You may require advice on a very broad range of issues, such as the size of a proposed project, important literature in the area that you are interested in and the **research question** that you seek to answer. Each of these areas, however,

Sketch note 4.1: Read the information

Sketch note 4.2: Don't forget to write things down

should be student–led: the student gives their ideas or concerns to the supervisor, who then considers them. Based on their experience and knowledge of previous dissertations, the supervisor suggests whether the idea is likely to fit within the scope of a dissertation project. In my experience, almost all student ideas need tweaking to make them feasible. This is often not because the student is 'wrong', but rather too ambitious.

You can ensure the guidance that you are given by your supervisor is most appropriate to your situation by being very clear during conversations. Short bullet-pointed lists of key elements can be helpful to bring to supervision or to share with your supervisor. Later (Chapters 9 and 12), we will discuss how **meaning** can easily be mis–constructed between **authors** and **readers**, and your communication with your supervisor is no different.

Skill development

Supervisors' roles in relation to developing your skills vary considerably between disciplines. Within dissertations that use documentary analysis, the skills that you are most likely to gain are searching for and retrieving documents from an **archive** or online space, cataloguing the documents that you collect, and undertaking analysis. These are skills that may be best tried yourself in advance of supervisory meetings, with questions, problems or comments brought to your supervisor's attention, as they are large and complex activities. Often, there are how–to guides available online that can point you in the right direction to make these explorations as fruitful as possible. You could ask your supervisor if there are particular books, papers or resources they would suggest you use, so that you have a shared understanding of the task you are performing.

Feedback on your progress

Reviewing work and providing feedback on your progress is a core supervisory activity in many dissertation programmes. Such feedback can be based on data that you have collected, a **sample** of your data analysis – such as reviewing your coding frame – and reviewing structures or draft chapters of your dissertation. Generally, a full draft of the dissertation will be reviewed and commented on *once only* prior to submission, and in some programmes a full draft will not be reviewed at all. In relation to reviewing your written work, supervisors may comment on 'big picture' content, such as the structure or language you have used, and how this impacts the clarity of your argument. For example, sometimes students use a lot of jargon and specialist terminology in their written work to show that they are familiar with it. However, this can cloud the **meaning** of your work, and simpler language may be more appropriate (see Becker (1986) for more details).

Supervisors may also comment on 'small picture' content, such as missing a key piece of research, attributing a point to the wrong researcher, or misunderstanding a point made in literature you are citing. Spelling and grammar are not routinely corrected by your supervisor, as this is outside the scope of supervision. If this is something you struggle with, see Chapter 13 for solutions.

Why are supervisor/supervisee relationships challenging?

As an undergraduate, the power differential between yourself and your supervisor can feel large. This can make voicing any concerns that you have feel uncomfortable or impossible. If your relationship with your supervisor is frustrating or challenging, you are not alone. Research on undergraduate students' and supervisors' experiences of working together to create a dissertation highlights a number of issues. Table 4.1 provides an overview of the research. By sharing this research, I hope to show you that tensions within the relationship are normal, rather than an individual issue related to you. Overall, the biggest and most common issues reported were lack of clarity, inconsistency and the power imbalance between supervisors and students. Knowing these common issues, you can plan in advance to mitigate the challenges.

Overcoming known challenges in supervisory relationships

I recommend that if you are undertaking your dissertation within a programme where you will have a lot of interaction with your supervisor, you take the time to become aware of your supervisor's preferences. A pro forma to record supervisory preferences can be found in Resource 4.1, with example responses within the Preferences and Notes columns. An unanswered version is available online as a resource.

Table 4.1: Students' and supervisors' views of undergraduate dissertation supervisory relationships

	Positive	Negative
Students' views of supervision	• Value autonomy • Appreciate the opportunity to 'validate' their learning through a dissertation • Appreciate the **authenticity** of doing their own research • Feeling of ownership over the work • Able to contribute to a good supervisory relationship through effort on project	• Feeling of uncertainty • Challenges of data collection • Time management
Students' views of supervisors	• Approachable • Available • Available for emotional support • Empowering • Directed learning • Interests aligned with the project	• Lack of clarity on next steps • Inconsistent advice, including relating to the marketing criteria • Power imbalances • Perceived inequalities in the amount of supervision given across students • Pressure to publish from supervisors, leading to feeling inadequate, and supervisors being uninterested in non-publishable data
Supervisors' views of their own supervision style	• Provide direct and clear advice • Instil confidence • Foster independence and growth	• Feel worried when they have to supervise a method they do not use (and do not have time to learn about)

Sources: Roberts and Seaman (2018), Todd et al (2004) and Wiggins et al (2016)

Sketch note 4.3: It's OK to ask questions

Resource 4.1: A pro forma to record your supervisor's preferences

Issue		Preference	Notes
Contact outside of meetings	Urgent issue	Phone – email if no answer	Mark email as urgent
	Routine update	Weekly email	Use numbers/bullet points for multiple issues
	Method to submit work	Email	In subject use CAPITAL LETTERS or similar
Contact about meetings	Pre-meeting agenda required?	Yes	Ideally a few days before
	Post-meeting notes required?	Yes	List supervisor actions in email too
Written work	Font	Sans serif based – size 12	
	Spacing	1.5 or double spaced	
	Margins	Wide	
References	Style	Harvard	
	Use of referencing software	No preference	Uses Mendeley
Technology	Sharing electronic analysis files	Yes	
	Use of analysis software	Uses Nvivo v12	Need to convert to Mac versions for her

How should I communicate with my supervisor?

Now we know the importance of supervisor–student communication, we move on to how best to communicate with your supervisor. Frustratingly, again, there is not a 'one size fits all' answer to this question. That said, in the context of your supervisor having (often very) limited time to support you in undertaking a dissertation, it is sensible for you to use your supervision time as efficiently as possible. It might help for you to consider your family and their communication styles: some people who only speak on the phone, others who cannot get off the phone quickly enough, those who message, and those who email only without verbal interaction. In Box 4.2 I describe my communication preferences and compare them to those of other supervisors.

Box 4.2: A range of supervisors' communication preferences

My personal preference would be for a dissertation student to email no more than once a week between supervisions, with a bullet-pointed list of questions/concerns/issues, *unless* they are having such a big problem that they feel they can't progress without my opinion. But that's me; I like quite a lot of details and a feeling that the project is going well, but not too much small talk.

Prof A prefers their students to telephone them the night before supervisions to briefly talk through issues, so any solutions can be thought about ahead of the meeting.

Dr B enjoys very friendly, jovial relationships with her students where laughter is often heard.

How can I lead the way in the supervisory relationship?

Regardless of your supervisor's particular communication preferences, one essential ingredient is being organised enough to have some understanding of the issues you are having with your dissertation, and where you would like your supervisor's support. Resource 4.2 is a supervision meeting planner that can be used in advance as an agenda, for issues you want to raise, and to briefly record notes to circulate to your supervisor after the meeting. You may not find this format suits your style of note-taking, so – as usual – do feel free to adapt it.

Resource 4.2: Supervision meeting planner

Topics	The specific issue	Important notes from the meeting	My actions	Date for completion	My supervisor's actions	Date for completion
E.g.: Finding literature on stigma and benefits for Disabled people	I can't find anything on WHEN Disabled people came to be seen by the UK government as 'scroungers'	A Conservative politician gave a lecture in the early 90s – there is a transcript and an article he wrote around the same time			Will search for the name of the politician and email me	By next Friday – email a reminder if he hasn't sent it by then

Sketch note 4.4: Always use version control

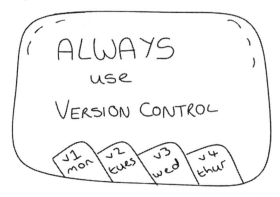

Don't lose information

Another element of organisation is storage of the information provided to you by your supervisors. This can be divided into three elements:

- Coming to supervisions ready to record the information your supervisor is giving you, either as notes, as typed words or, with their prior agreement, via a recording device. It is not the supervisor's responsibility to do this unless you have a specific learning difficulty and an agreed statement of reasonable adjustments from disability services.
- You may need to go away and expand on these notes soon after the meeting, in order to provide additional context around what was said, or to make a note of your actions (which you then do ahead of their agreed deadline) or any actions that your supervisor asked that you remind them of.
- Your supervisor may provide information electronically, such as relevant articles or feedback on your draft chapters, and you should ensure that you store and review this information. Setting up folders in your cloud-based storage *and at least one back-up of these*, and another folder within your emails that is only for your dissertation, can be one way of making sure that you do not lose any of this information.

Feeding back after meetings

One area that is often neglected is the practice of students taking the notes that they have made in meetings and typing them up into notes that they then keep themselves and also email to their supervisor. This enables the supervisor to skim the notes – which should be relatively brief – to ensure that shared understanding has occurred. The notes should include the important decisions that were made, the actions the student needs to undertake and the deadline for each action, and any actions and deadlines for the supervisor. This record of your supervisory meetings is very helpful when you are writing up and cannot remember why particular decisions were made, or if your supervisor is ill and you are allocated another supervisor.

Deadlines

A particular bugbear of supervisors is students submitting drafts of work later than agreed, without providing sufficient (or sometimes any) advanced warning. If your supervisor has told you that they need to receive your written work two weeks prior to your meeting, and you send it over to them a few days before the meeting, their other commitments may well mean that they do not have time to engage as comprehensively as they would have liked.

What if I can't make my supervisory relationship work?

The statement 'it takes two to tango' applies to supervisory relationships; yes, you as the junior partner are required to undertake the lion's share of the work, but your supervisor does need to contribute. If you feel that things are not working as well as they could, you may wish to consider the steps in Figure 4.1. My advice is to avoid the 'nuclear option' of a formal complaint unless it is absolutely necessary (e.g. due to harassment, discrimination or assault of some kind). You can attempt to regain control and get the outcome that you want by politely reminding them of the outstanding action ahead of your next supervision. If that doesn't work, consider whether it is essential for the thing to be done as soon as possible; is your deadline looming (either to submit or for an ethics committee)? If not, can you afford to wait until your next supervision and then bring up the missing thing and their communication preferences? If you feel that you need support immediately due to the extreme urgency of your need, or your supervisor's continuing lack of engagement, it may be time to either informally or formally discuss the matter with another member of staff.

Those who can support you in this will vary from institution to institution and could include the administrators in charge of your degree as a whole or your year group, or the module convenor for dissertations. A non-confrontational approach would be to say that your supervisor is unreachable and ask if they know if your supervisor is on leave and when they will be back. If you get to the point where you feel that there is no hope for your supervisory relationship, it may be time to involve the official complaints procedure in your department; details should be included in your dissertation module handbook or online learning portal. Cases that would be appropriate to consider here include where you are unable to contact your supervisor for a long time (relative to the size of your project and how much time you have prior to submitting) with no advanced notice; where you feel that the supervisor is bullying you, harassing you in some way (sexual advances, racist or ableist comments, etc.); or where the supervisor

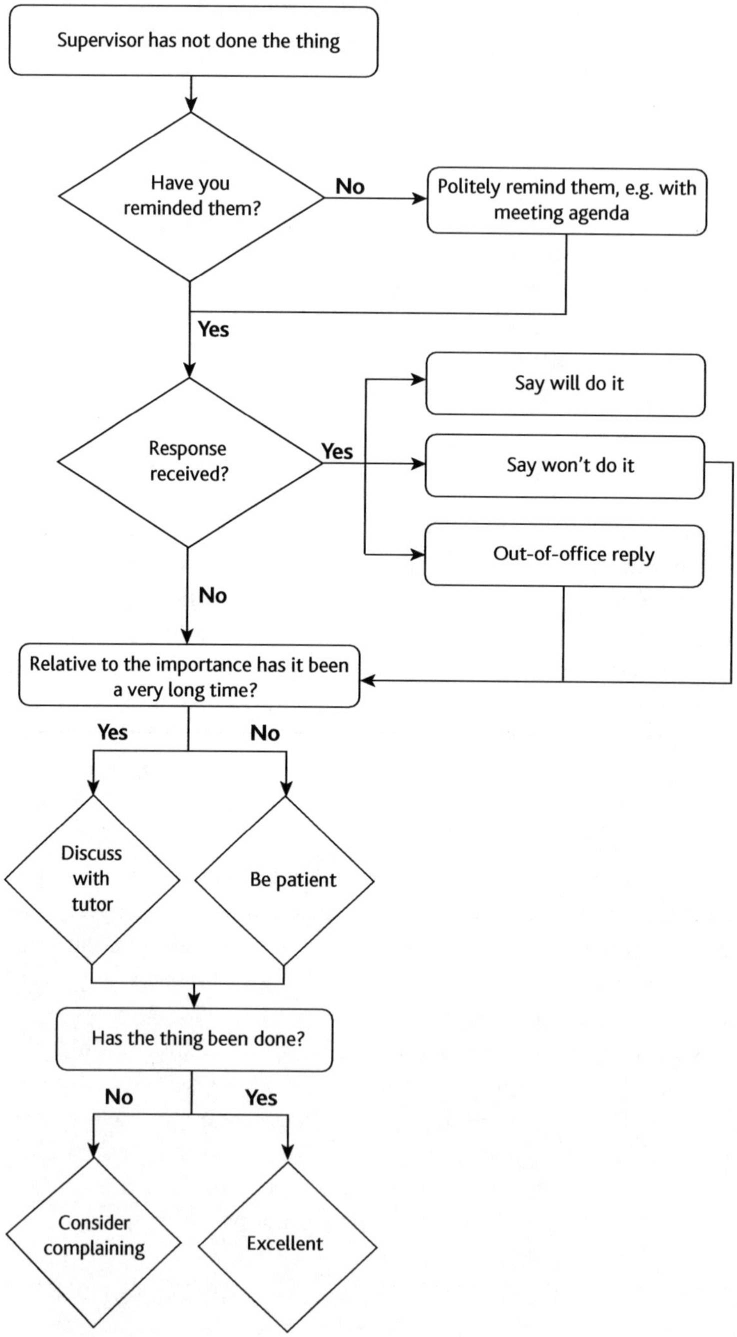

Figure 4.1: Flow chart – my supervisor isn't doing what they said they would

has consistently not carried out their role in relation to the guidance in your department's dissertation handbook.

Conclusion

One common issue relating to student dissatisfaction within their dissertation is that their supervisor is not supporting them as they think they should. This frustration and conflict within a relationship with a clear power hierarchy is never going to benefit the less powerful individual (the student). Instead, in this chapter, I introduced you to ways to hopefully improve communication. If these techniques aren't helpful, I have provided guidance on informal and formal complaints.

Further reading

Undergraduate

Anonymous (2017, 18 Dec.) 'Making the most of the relationship with your dissertation supervisor', *Nursing Times* [online]. Available at: www.nursingtimes. net/roles/nurse-educators/making-the-most-of-the-relationship-with-your-dissertation-supervisor-18-12-2017/ [Accessed 18 December 2020].

Boynton, P. (2017) 'How to email someone about your research', *The Research Companion* [online]. Available at: https://theresearchcompanion.com/resear chemail/ [Accessed 18 December 2020].

Postgraduate

Anonymous (2016, 17 Aug.) 'Working with your PhD supervisor', *FindaPhD. com* [online]. Available at: www.findaphd.com/advice/doing/you-and-your-phd-supervisor.aspx [Accessed 18 December 2020].

Delamont, S., Atkinson, P. and Parry, O. (2004) *Supervising the Doctorate*, Milton Keynes: Open University Press.

Pugh, D. and Estelle, P. (2015) *How to Get a PhD: A Handbook for Students and Supervisors*, Milton Keynes: Open University Press, pp 76–94.

Working ethically

Summary

In this section, you will be asked to consider the ethical code or codes that you will follow during your dissertation. However, this is only the first step: you will then be invited to consider data protection laws, your university's good conduct policy and also 'The *Daily Mail* Test'; that is, would your research design and practice look bad if it was reported by the **tabloid** media? Alongside guidance on how to do your research without causing harm, this chapter is also the place where inclusive scholarship, or moving away from *only* citing old white men, is described. The purpose of this chapter is to highlight that working ethically isn't something that is a one-off box-ticking exercise, but something to consider throughout each stage of your dissertation.

Objectives

By reading this chapter, you should understand:

- what ethical principles are, and how they apply in documentary research;
- how to choose which ethical code(s) to follow;
- why inclusive ethics, design, and citation practices matter.

Introduction: The blurred line between real life and documentary lives

The time available to develop dissertations and other research projects is almost always less than ideal. Thinking has to be done quickly, and dead ends may be encountered before finding suitable data. For this reason, it may be inconvenient to consider the ethical issues in using data that are *available* to be collected. However, we really must make time for this, not only because of the importance of ethics themselves but also because your examiners will be assessing your research design and conduct based on this.

Research with pre-existing documents is often seen as ethically uncomplicated. If the documents are in the public domain, it can be argued, they are 'fair game' for researchers. Similarly, if documents are in an **archive**, the fact that the researcher can access them may lead to a sense of security in relation to ethics. However, this is false. We now have robust rules and ethical procedures for undertaking observations in public spaces. This is a far cry from invasive observations of the past, such as Humphreys' (1970) *Tearoom Trade*, where the PhD student purposely observed gay sexual encounters in public toilets, at a time when homosexuality was illegal. The unethical acts further included keeping car registration numbers, which could have incriminated the men who were unknowingly under study. These days, that sort of study would not get through ethical review. However, if a similar study looked at, for example, an online community associated with illegal but consensual sexual acts (such as sadomasochistic sex in England and Wales, at the time of writing) and the data they mined contained IP addresses, a similar ethical breach will have occurred. As more and more of our lives are lived online, it is unethical to simply observe and '**mine**' (the term used for collecting large volumes of online data, often from social media) people's information uncritically.

What ethical principles do I need to consider?

In this section, we consider ethical principles from professional codes of practice, ethical advisory groups, and also our own moral codes. These factors are summarised in Box 5.1 and each of the bullet points in the box is elaborated on below. An example of ethical reflections within a PhD dissertation can be seen in Box 5.2. In the study, Mustafa (2015) used case study research, including documentary analysis within the context of an Islamic state with strict gender rules. He followed the rules required in order to undertake the research, but also reflected on his own levels of ethical appropriateness, erring on the side of caution.

Box 5.1: Checklist: thinking about ethics within your research design and practice

If you had to be completely honest about it, does the research you are thinking of doing feel ethically sound in relation to:

- your own feelings about appropriateness;
- data protection or privacy laws;
- professional codes of ethics;
- your university or organisation's codes;
- public opinion ('The *Daily Mail* Test').

If the answer to any of these is *no*, or *I don't know*, you need to undertake further reading and reflection.

Box 5.2: Student example: ethical considerations within a case study of gender within a modernising Islamic state (Mustafa, 2015)

In his fascinating research on gender and leisure within Saudi society, Majed Mustafa used four data collection methods, including documentary analysis of pre-existing media content and observation in leisure spaces. He notes that: 'The sensitivity of gender relationships was a major factor in the ethical approach, and also shaped and limited, in some respects, the field investigation' (p 52). As part of data collection within leisure spaces such as malls and theme parks, Mustafa took photographs to analyse as data. However, this was not ethically straightforward, and required approval from local police departments as well as the owners/ managers of the private spaces that he was collecting data within, and that furthermore he avoided taking photos 'in crowded spaces especially with the presence of females' (p 52). He notes that this impacted upon the data collected and, accordingly, the conclusions identified.

It is important that you keep in mind that the considerations noted in Box 5.1 relate to *all* processes within your dissertation; the literature you exclude from your review (see Chapter 7); the decision to use particular data (see Chapter 8); and the **research question** this leads you to (see Chapter 10). Furthermore, the theoretical framework you choose to work within (see Chapter 2), and your own **positionality** and how it aligns with that of the **authors** of your documents (see Chapter 6) are central to ethical practice. To help you collect your thoughts about ethical issues, you may wish to use – or amend – Resource 5.1, which is also available online.

Your own feelings about appropriateness

When we are undertaking research, there is a tension between research that is important because the participants are vulnerable, and research that is exploitative because the participants are vulnerable, *especially* if they didn't consent to their content being used in a study. At the time of writing, there was a forum or social media group dedicated to each rare disease, social problem and specialist interest group. Just because these pieces of information are available for you to read, does not mean that participants of the group are expecting a researcher to come along and analyse their innermost thoughts. I would encourage you to avoid getting carried away by sensationalist online content unless there is a strong argument for studying that topic, because of the potential to cause harm.

It could be suggested that the question to consider here is 'would you like this done to you?' However, your own privilege (see Chapter 6) may well vary from that of the **authors** of the documents you are considering using as data. Alongside

Resource 5.1: Considering ethical issues in your dissertation

Thing to consider	Topic	Thoughts	Next steps
My thoughts on what is morally right			
Data protection laws, etc.			
University's code			
Professional body's code			
Public opinion: 'The *Daily Mail* test'			

Box 5.3: Ethics, covert data collection and harm: ways to study students' views

Within their research on the reasons that engineering students leave their programme, Whitehair and Berdanier (2018) mined data from anonymous social media posts. This approach was justified because the data allowed for a holistic view of *how* programmes could be improved, and students were not identifiable. By contrast, Rachel Syring Ryan (2013) investigated how students experienced the use of online learning environments containing discussion forums through a questionnaire, rather than through mining the data produced within the online learning environment itself. It may be that Ryan never considered using documentary analysis, due to a positivistic research paradigm. Furthermore, ethics and consent were not discussed at all within the dissertation, so it is not that one approach was more ethical than the other, but simply that good research ethics take planning.

this, the potential harm to the **authors** of the documents could be considerable. As such, it is important to not be oblivious to structural inequalities in society when considering harm. For instance, if you are white, and researching Black or Indigenous perspectives, you must keep in mind that you are far less likely to be criminalised for a routine matter. In such an instance, it is important to read about research ethics in relation to the marginalised group under study. Box 5.4 notes relevant further reading relating to research with marginalised groups.

Box 5.4: Resources for ethical research practice with marginalised groups

- Age – Swartz, S. (2011) '"Going deep" and "giving back": strategies for exceeding ethical expectations when researching amongst vulnerable youth', *Qualitative Research*, 11(1): 47–68.
- Disability – Bridges, D. (2017) *Philosophy in Educational Research*, Springer: New York. Chapter 20: '"Nothing about us without us": the ethics of outsider research', pp 341–361.
- Economic status (social class) – Burchardt, T. (2014) 'Deliberative research as a tool to make value judgements', *Qualitative Research*, 14(3): 353–370.
- Gender – Edwards, R. and Mauthner, M. (2021) 'Ethics and feminist research: theory and practice', in Mauthner, M., Birch, M., Jessop, J. and Miller, T. (eds) *Ethics in Qualitative Research* (2nd edn), London: Sage, pp 14–28.
- Neurodiversity – Fletcher-Watson, S., Adams, J., Brook, K. et al (2018) 'Making the future together: shaping autism research through meaningful participation', *Autism*, 23(4): 943–953.

- Race and ethnicity – Zuberi, T. and Bonilla-Silva, E. (2008) *White Logic, White Methods: Racism and Methodology*, Rowman & Littlefield: Plymouth.
- Sexuality – Wagle, T. and Cantaffa, D.T. (2008) 'Working our hyphens: exploring identity relations in qualitative research', *Qualitative Inquiry*, 14(1): 135–159.

Sketch note 5.1: Read widely

University codes of ethical conduct

Each university, and sometimes each department within a university, will have their own set of ethical rules. If you breach these rules, you could theoretically be removed from your course, the university could be sued by any participants that are harmed, and the university and/or your department could suffer significant reputational damage. These are all obviously things that could have serious consequences for your life and future job prospects. So, how can we ensure that we do not breach these codes? A summary of the processes involved in making sure you do not breach your university's guidelines can be found in Figure 5.1. The most important thing is to familiarise yourself with the

Figure 5.1: How to stay within your university's ethical code

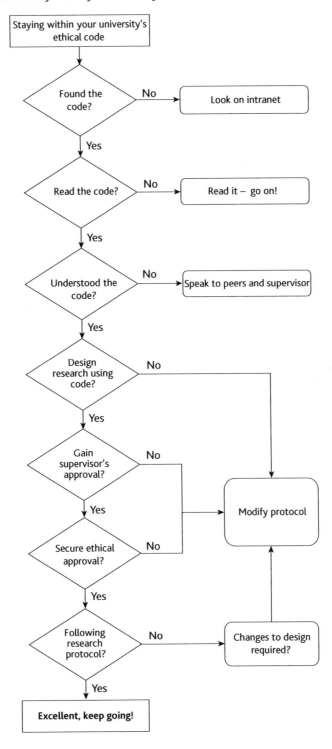

ethical guidance. You can usually find this on your department's intranet. Once you have found the code, which may be several pages long, often having the documents required to gain ethical approval within them, you need to ensure that you understand it.

In this instance, there are two types of understanding: intellectually understanding what the words mean and (critically) understanding how to put those words into practice within your research project. Starting with intellectually understanding the code, you may wish to begin with the forms that researchers need to complete for ethical review. These forms often have tick boxes, which highlight ethical risks within studies. Common questions include considering if you are undertaking research with a vulnerable group, such as children, prisoners, or those who are unable to give their informed consent. Methodologically, ethical approval forms are often constructed as though research is going to be undertaken with interaction between the researcher and participant. This is often not the case in documentary analysis, and you may need to ask your supervisor how to tailor your responses appropriately.

In some circumstances, researchers who use documents in their research are exempt from their university's ethical review procedures. If this is the case in your university, I strongly recommend that you make a list of potential harms from your research and discuss them with your supervisor prior to beginning your project. This ensures that should anything go wrong with your research, there is a clear record (from your notes, which you emailed to your supervisor after the session) that you went above and beyond the required minimum of your department.

Staying within the law

Your university's code of ethics has likely considered data protection and privacy laws in your country of study. That said, it is still worth spending time familiarising yourself with the details relating to using data, to ensure you fully understand your responsibilities. For example, within the European Union, researchers are treated in the same way as other organisations and are subjected to the rules contained within the EU General Data Protection Regulation (GDPR). If you are unsure about the laws that you must operate within, you should ask your supervisor.

Alongside this, although they are not laws, some social media platforms and internet forums provide rules for researchers who want to use content from that website. For example, at the time of writing, Twitter insisted that opt-in consent should occur before content is reproduced verbatim, and Mumsnet states that forum content should not be used in research. Instead, they ask that researchers pay a small fee and begin their own discussion within a forum post, clearly marking that it is a research project. If you plan to collect data online, search for the website's policy on research before committing to using those data.

Sketch note 5.2: Don't forget to write things down

Professional bodies' ethical codes

Within the social sciences and humanities, there are a wide range of professional bodies. It may be that your course and your supervisor are expecting you to work within a particular professional code. In some subjects, it will be obvious which professional body you should align yourself with. For example, psychology degree programmes in the UK require supervisors and procedures validated by the British Psychological Society (BPS). By contrast, within social policy, many undergraduates may not be aware of the Social Policy Association. If you are required to work within a professional body's code of ethics, it should be clear in your dissertation handbook.

Sketch note 5.3: Don't break data protection laws

One group that is worthy of mention in this book is the Association of Internet Researchers (AoIR). The AoIR is a collective of researchers who use data found or generated online. They have a code of ethical guidelines for those using data from the internet (franzke et al, 2020), and have been a critical voice in relation to the ethical implications of data mining. They state that there are 'judgement calls … not recipes' in relation to internet research. If you are using online content as your data, I highly recommend consulting the AoIR code of ethics.

'The Daily Mail Test'

The *Daily Mail* is a **tabloid** newspaper from the UK that has been criticised for publishing views that many find racist, sexist and bigoted (Balch and Balabanova, 2017). 'The *Daily Mail* Test' is used as shorthand to describe how the public would view something – such as a policy change or pay rise for a director of a large organisation – if it were in the public domain. As a researcher I use 'The *Daily Mail* Test' to consider how the findings of my research could be used to damage the reputation of the **authors** of the documents used as data. In Box 5.5, research on mothers' views of homework for young children is described, showing the steps taken by the researcher to ensure privacy and to protect participants from harm. If you are concerned about how your research could be reported, and any impact on the **authors** of the documents that you have used, you *must* take steps to anonymise the data.

Sketch note 5.4: Don't lose your integrity

> **Box 5.5: Case study: primary school homework – good mother, bad mother (Lehner-Mear, 2020)**
>
> Research by Rachel Lehner-Mear (2020) mined online parenting communities to explore views and attitudes relating to primary school homework, with a **discourse analysis** approach used in order to understand attitudes regarding good and bad motherhood. Within the paper, the **author** chose to anonymise the names of the two online communities from which she collected her data, calling them

'*MothersChat*' and '*MaternalNatter*'. Furthermore, direct quotations were not used unless they were commonly used phrases. In doing so, the researcher ensured that the privacy of the individuals who had posted in these open access forums was protected. You may wish to adopt a similar approach, particularly if your research topic is contentious.

Inclusive citation, ethics and design

At the time of writing, it was still very common for older white men to flourish as academics, while women, Disabled people and those from marginalised groups had their research considered less favourably. In Chapter 7 on constructing your literature review, we will talk more about ensuring the literature that informs your **research question** comes from a range of perspectives. Now, we briefly consider how research ethics can be white-centric and focused on western value systems, which impacts on research design, data generation and conclusions.

In recent decades, there has been a move to decolonise research ethics, acknowledging the harm of powerful groups investigating marginalised groups, particularly when it comes to obtaining social justice (see, for example, Jolivette, 2015). This includes a broader definition of ethics, and more consideration of integrity than what is required by many ethical approval committees. When we do not read methods literature from outside our own privileged circle, we can fail to take account of the lived experience of the people writing the documents we analyse. Accordingly, it is good practice to at least be aware of the connections between discrimination and ethics. *White logic, white methods* (Zuberi and Bonilla-Silva, 2008) is an excellent 'all-rounder' book that is essential reading if you are undertaking research on a marginalised racial or ethnic group. If you are looking for something more specific, Helen Kara has an excellent **blog**, where she prioritises citing marginalised researchers and regularly updates a reading list on decolonising methods (Kara, 2020).

I am coming to understand that I still have much to learn in relation to racism, and other minority groups. Very few people reading this book will not have any privilege, and it is our duty as ethical researchers to consider our privilege and its potential effects. For example, our research can stigmatise: we might become part of the problem we are trying to highlight.

Conclusion

This chapter has discussed research ethics from a range of angles, to allow you to decide how to approach the area within your dissertation research project. To ensure rigorous ethical practice, consider *a broad definition of ethics* in your research design and practice. First, do you really, truly believe that your research plan is ethical? If yes, consider your plan in relation to your university's ethical approval process, relevant laws (particularly focused on privacy and data security) and how the research could affect the group under study if it was reported in the media. If all of that feels OK, it is time to draft your ethical approval documents and your study protocol or methods chapter (whichever is required in your department). You will then need to keep these issues in mind as you undertake your research; ethics is not a moment, but a process. As we began to discuss, assessment of your **positionality** goes hand-in-hand with being an ethical researcher. The next chapter focuses on **positionality** and **reflexivity** and how to use them in your dissertation in more detail.

Further reading

Undergraduate

Bonilla-Silva, E. and Baiocchi, G. (2008) 'Anything but racism: how sociologists limit the significance of racism', in T. Zuberi and E. Bonilla-Silva (eds) *White Logic, White Methods: Racism and Methodology,* Plymouth: Rowman & Littlefield, pp 137–152.

franzke, a., Bechmann, A., Zimmer, M., Ess, C. and the Association of Internet Researchers (2020) 'Internet research: ethical guidelines 3.0, Association of Internet Researchers' [online] 6 October 2019. Available at: https://aoir.org/ethics/ [Accessed 21 December 2020].

Kara, H. (2018a) *Research Ethics in the Real World: Euro-western and Indigenous Perspectives,* Bristol: Policy Press, pp 71–85.

Largan, C. and Morris, T. (2019) *Qualitative Secondary Research: A Step by Step Guide,* London: SAGE, pp 99–120.

Postgraduate

Israel, M. (2014) *Research Ethics and Integrity for Social Scientists: Beyond Regulatory Compliance,* London: SAGE.

Kara, H. (2020, 29 July) 'Decolonising methods', *Helen Kara blog* [online]. Available at: https://helenkara.com/2020/07/29/decolonising-methods-a-reading-list/ [Accessed 27 February 2020].

Mertens, D.M. and Ginsberg, P.E. (2009) *The Handbook of Social Research Ethics,* London: SAGE.

Zuberi, T. and Bonilla-Silva, E. (2008) *White Logic, White Methods: Racism and Methodology,* Plymouth: Rowman & Littlefield.

6

Working reflexively and safely

Summary

Positionality refers to your impact on the research because of your demographics and experiences, and **reflexivity** (which is increasingly viewed as essential when undertaking research) is the process of assessing one's **positionality**. You may be new to the concept of **positionality**; it may not have been covered in your research methods teaching to date, especially if your course has a positivistic lens on the construction of knowledge. However, ethical practice and **reflexivity** go hand in hand; you cannot have one without the other. In this chapter, I provide a rationale for its importance in documentary analysis. Alongside this, I introduce you to practical tools to facilitate your **reflexive** thinking, including interrogating your own thoughts and reactions through the regular use of a research diary. The chapter ends by considering the role of self-care within research, which can often contain emotive data, and provides strategies to facilitate the provision and receipt of support from your peers.

Objectives

By reading this chapter, you should understand:

- what **reflexivity** and **positionality** are;
- how to be **reflexive** in your work;
- what a research diary (sometimes known as a field diary) is;
- why self-care is important, especially if you have upsetting data.

Introduction: Why you really shouldn't skip this chapter

While it is likely most dissertation students will have heard of ethics and ethical review, some of you will be unfamiliar with the terms **positionality** and **reflexivity**. I imagine that few **readers** will feel fully confident to consider their position in the research process and document it for their dissertation. Increasingly, assessments of **reflexivity** are a standard part of the methods chapter

Sketch note 6.1: Demographics + experience = positionality

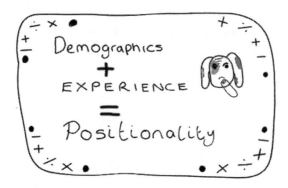

of social science dissertations, and they are sometimes expected in the strengths and limitations section of the discussion chapter.

When I was first introduced to these concepts, I believed that they were much more complicated – and frightening – than they really are. To be reflexive, to be aware of your demographics and the privileges they bring, spend time considering your views and experiences in relation to the topic of your research, and do this throughout the research process. Within this chapter, I will introduce you to tools to help you consider your own **positionality**. Undertaking research on sensitive topics or becoming more aware of social injustice can be emotionally demanding. For this reason, at the end of the chapter you will find self-care strategies that you can apply to yourself, but also to friends and peers.

What are reflexivity and positionality?

Over the past 30 years, there has been increasing recognition that researchers should be **reflexive**. What this means in practice is that researchers should be aware of, and declare, their **epistemology** and **ontology**: that is, the basis on which they draw their understanding of the world. This includes the research paradigm (e.g. **interpretivist** vs. **positivist**) that you subscribe to, and any **theory** that you are using to frame your research. Regardless of your theoretical perspective, it is necessary to consider the social and political structures around and interacting with us, and the events of our own lives. We then consider how these different elements intersect and then apply that to why we think or do particular things within our research. Our research, at its most basic, is seeking to compare, and the research that you undertake using one set of documents and a particular **research question** may uncover different findings to that of a researcher with a different background. Within an **interpretivist** approach, this is viewed as inevitable, and it is therefore undesirable to pretend that the research will lead to one single truth (because

Box 6.1: Student example: reflexivity in the feminist study of institutions (Murray, 2018)

In Orla Murray's dissertation, which draws on Dorothy Smith's brilliant Institutional Ethnography approach to documentary analysis (see Smith and Turner, 2014), she considers her **ontology**, **epistemology** and positionality in relation to her feminist research paradigm, by asking 'What constitutes feminist research?' (p 74). For Murray, the answer is to be thorough in her consideration of both **epistemology** and reflexivity. She notes (pp 74–77):

- Intersectional feminism – that is, considering other marginalised identities, not just a shared gender – is important.
- Being a feminist oneself is not enough to make your research design feminist.
- It is not possible, within feminist paradigms, to create knowledge in a neutral way: '[a] feminist approach to research cannot just add women and stir, but rather must fundamentally challenge the presumption of an objective, detached researcher whose epistemic privilege is unable to be challenged by those he researches' (p 75).
- Being attuned to the power relationships between researcher and researched is essential.
- Researchers must reflect on the relationships and rapport between the researcher and participants.

Within her research, she notes that she was reflexive not just in terms of writing about her positionality, but by actively reflecting on sharing it with participants. She describes this and how it impacted on her relationships with participants in some piloting she undertook: 'I shared many identity categories with my participants (gender, race and often sexuality and class) alongside also being from Belfast and identifying as a feminist, which meant that I found it easy to gain access to feminist circles and developed good rapport with some of the activists' (p 7). By contrast, she does not consider her similarity in relation to, for example, hobbies, motherhood status, transport choice or many other areas which are less relevant to her positionality in this study.

for interpretivists there is no one single truth). Box 6.1 presents an example of how a PhD student used reflexivity in their documentary analysis study, which utilised a feminist research paradigm.

How can I be reflexive?

Asking yourself questions at the outset

Box 6.1 highlights a primary area in which **positionality** was important to that project. In any project, an assessment of **positionality** will need to be bespoke to that project, with more emphasis given to the ways in which you are or are not closely related to the topic. This is because the assumptions in your **research question** and analysis will likely be about different topics in different projects. Resource 6.1, which is also available online for you to use or amend, provides a structure for considering your positionality in relationship to the **author(s)** of your documents and their intended **reader(s)**. As you can see from Box 6.1, it is not necessary to fully explore each area in a large amount of detail. However, sometimes as projects continue, it becomes clear that elements of your personal characteristics that you had not considered in detail were worthy of further thought, so it is worth briefly checking back on your positionality each time you read a new piece of literature or consider a piece of data. An easy way to do this is through keeping a research diary (see below).

By using tools like Resource 6.1 and keeping a research diary, what you are really looking to achieve is an assessment of how similar your interpretation of the language and **meaning** would be to those of the **author** and the **reader**. As we will consider in Chapter 9, most analysis of documents will involve an assessment of what the **author** hoped the **reader** would understand from it. This includes the use of words that can seem neutral or factual, but in reality are intended to convey a particular message; either positive or negative. One way of assessing how likely you are to be able to read the **meaning** intended is to consider how much of an 'insider' or 'outsider' you are, based on your responses to Resource 6.1, or the notes that you are keeping in your research diary in relation to your positionality relative to the **authors**, intended **readers** and the documents themselves. The concept of insider/outsider positionality originates from the work of Howard Becker; for an overview of how it has been used, see Kersen (2016). Box 6.2 provides an example of a researcher assessing their status in relation to this dichotomy.

Research diaries

Typically, the use of research diaries or field notes is associated with the tradition of ethnographic research. They are, however, valuable as a tool to help you understand your changing views of the data – these are your early analytical thoughts – and their influences from your **positionality**. Furthermore, they can be used to help you work through your emotional responses to the data. I would encourage researchers to be brutally honest in their field notes, knowing that nobody else need see them (including their supervisor) without permission. In fact, I sometimes encourage students to keep one 'clean' and one 'full' set of notes; one becomes the 'memory' of the project, while the other is there as a 'brain dump'. Keeping a field diary can feel odd at first, particularly when it is

Resource 6.1: Considering positionality

Concept	Current	Historical	Impact re: authorship	Impact re: (intended) readership
Age				
Class				
Disability				
Education				
Ethnicity				
Gender				
Gender identity				
Home ownership				
Income				
Nationality				
Neurodiversity				
Religion				
Sexuality				
Wealth				

Box 6.2: Are you an insider or an outsider (or somewhere in between)?

To determine your status as 'similar to' (insider) or 'not similar to' (outsider), you can consider the various ways in which you are aligned with the **author** or **reader** of your documents. Often it is not clear cut. In *Changing Digital Geographies: Technologies, Environments and People*, Jessica McLean (2020) presents a range of case studies relating to how digital technologies are used to communicate (i.e. create documents). Within her research, she describes attending a conference on 'Human Rights and Technology', including her **positionality** within the event. She notes that the fee was high, and that she was unsure if she could attend (showing lower socio-economic status than other presenters or being a more junior academic, perhaps), as the venue was 'an expensive hotel on the Sydney Harbour' (p 47). Furthermore, McLean notes that it was unclear which *technology* and which *human rights* would be discussed in advance, as the pre-conference written materials were ambiguous, showing a broad range of 'technology', which highlighted the potential of being an 'outsider' based on her expertise. A range of corporate sponsors were involved, and this introduced accessibility to the conference in the form of captioning, and questions after each presenter being submitted digitally and voted on by the audience, which suggests a level of consideration of marginalised groups within the conference setting. An official welcome from a 'hospitable Indigenous elder' (p 48) resulted in McLean reflecting on the cultural context of ongoing colonial harms in Australia, which breach human rights.

Based on her account, McLean can be viewed as mostly an 'insider' in relation to the conference and its associated materials; she is an expert on the topic and is able to afford the fee. She feels comfortable in the expensive environment, but also acknowledges the 'price' of the colonial development to Indigenous locals. Furthermore, attempts to make the materials accessible and democratic prioritised inclusion of those who are often marginalised.

you writing your thoughts about what you are reading. If you are struggling with your diary, a change of medium may help. Resource 6.2 is a template that you can use to help you start keeping your research diary if a blank page is difficult for you to respond to. As always, feel free to modify it, or simply take the bits that you find useful and leave the others behind. Please remember, there is no right way to keep a research diary. The blank template will be available online.

In Box 6.3 I describe the 'messy' way that my research diary is constructed. I've included this because, as a student, the process of academic writing was alien to me, and I was worried that I was 'doing it wrong' if I wasn't typing

Sketch note 6.2: Research diaries are your friends

into a word processing document or writing in my 'best' handwriting. Neither of these strategies worked; I preferred to write by hand, but I can't do legible handwriting for long *and* not interrupt my thoughts while doing it, as I write too slowly to keep up with the speed of my thoughts. Thankfully, Sara Delamont, an eminent and frankly awesome researcher, and the **author** of many amazing books on qualitative research (including *Supervising the Doctorate* (Delamont et al, 2004), which is useful for PhD and master's students as well as their supervisors, and Ward and Delamont (2020) focused on qualitative methods), described how she preferred to write new material on 'scrap' paper. Knowing this freed me up to write my research diary. I outline the style that I use for my research diary in Box 6.3. It's absolutely fine for you to change your mind about *how* you keep research diary notes, as long as you don't lose any information.

What should I do if I have an emotional response to the data?

Don't panic: this is completely normal. It has long been acknowledged that aspects of qualitative research can be harmful to the researcher, both in terms of emotional burden and also physical threat and violence. Often, doing research remotely on pre-existing documents is seen as not harmful to the researcher. We could theorise that this is because the documents exist in the past, and the researcher exists in the present. Alternatively, collecting data face-to-face is a multi-sensory, fully embodied experience, while words are on the page; the **authors** do not see you. This may mean that researchers who feel an emotional response to the documents they are working on internalise the harm that the research is doing to them. Because the emotional burden of doing this sort of research is little discussed, this may also mean that supervisors provide less support in the form of debriefing than they might to students who are collecting data face to face.

It is a fallacy that seeing written words on a page cannot harm you (Grant, 2018). The topics that we research are often topics that are of great importance to society, involving health, education, housing and homelessness, living conditions, and poverty. Research funding is often focused on addressing societies' big problems. This is where supervisors' areas of interest often lie, and thus dissertation projects that are interesting to the student and within supervisors' areas of expertise are

Resource 6.2: Getting started with your research diary

Date	Activity (reading, analysis, writing, etc.)	Thoughts	Next steps
E.g.: 3/12/20	Reading: Helen Kara Research Ethics in the Real World	Indigenous research methods = useful when aiming to have more equal power relations, but often neglected. Researcher wellbeing is also often neglected.	Make sure to read the rest of the book, Chp8 = sampling section of methods; Chp9 = analysis section of methods.
		When reviewing social media posts on waterpipe smoking must remember that it is usually associated with Arabic heritage.	Read up on the **cultural** significance of waterpipe smoking – what is the norm away from the Euro-centric nightclubs?

Box 6.3: Get it written, not right – my research diary process

I dictate the majority of my formal written work. However, I rarely dictate ad hoc field notes (compared to, for example, a full day of ethnographic data collection). My field diary begins (and sometimes ends) on sticky notes. As I'm going through documents that are my data, familiarising myself with their contents ahead of the formal analysis, I will write notes, perhaps sticking them to parts of printed extracts or just simply noting my thoughts and sticking them on the desk with a number at the top of each one to keep my thoughts in order. Sometimes I use several pads of sticky notes at the same time. I start writing my research diary on sticky notes because I generally think "there's not going to be much to think about here", or "I don't have anything 'clever' to say about this"; it feels less risky to my academic sense of self to not write in a 'proper' diary. This then means at the end of my session, I have plenty of prompts that I can write about, and I can also just stick entire chains of notes into my research diary if they are understandable as they are – I usually don't overlap them, so I can easily follow the flow of my thoughts later.

The second stage of writing my research diary, when I think something is going to be important, is to go from these notes to writing full sentences or bullet-pointed notes that I know will definitely make sense to me in six months. I prefer to write my research diary by hand, into a notebook. I am increasingly trying to get myself into the habit of dictating my research diary into my computer, as this means I can do things like sit holding a cup of tea as I 'write', which serves the dual purpose of reducing hand pain through less typing and heat and allowing me to hold my rough notes in my hand as I speak my thoughts.

often contentious. Having an emotional response is completely normal for qualitative researchers (see Dickson–Swift et al (2009) for a study of researchers' emotional responses to data).

How can I take care of my mental health while doing a dissertation?

Feel the emotion

Books aimed at undergraduate research methods students often exclude emotion. This is also the case in many of the journal articles that you will have read (see Loughran and Mannay (2018) for an exploration of this phenomenon). It is not surprising that undergraduates might believe that to be a researcher they have

Sketch note 6.3: How are you feeling?

to leave their compassion, empathy and emotion behind. Instead, I urge you to allow yourself to acknowledge your feelings. These feelings can be important because having an emotional reaction to something may mean something for your analysis. For example, if something makes you angry or sad, it may be because you perceive an injustice has happened to the **author** or the people they are talking about.

Reflect as you analyse

When you are doing your analysis, I suggest that you include emotional reactions in your research diary, and make sure to save these early notes: they can be very helpful later on. At first, considering emotional responses to your work can feel uncomfortable, because it is often unusual. In many societies, particularly the global North, we are taught from a young age to be compliant and to ignore our emotions. Many of our academic disciplines were founded on positivistic approaches, where the influence of the researcher was supposed to be minimised as much as possible. In qualitative research, we know that this approach is seriously flawed. Instead, we use **reflexivity**, a concept of analysing our own role in designing studies, collecting data and interpreting it. If it takes you a while to get used to using **reflexivity** in your research, you will not be unusual, and you are not expected to be an expert at this stage.

Peer support

While keeping a research diary can be extremely valuable, it may be inadequately supportive when you find yourself distressed by the data you are working with and/or the process of undertaking your dissertation. You may find it valuable to identify a support buddy or even a group of support buddies. This will enable both of you to debrief with somebody with whom you can discuss things that are too uncomfortable, or feel too difficult to articulate, to write in your field diary. Box 6.4 shows how formal dissertation support groups worked in one university.

Box 6.4: Dissertation support groups at the University of North Carolina, Charlotte, NC, USA (Russell-Pinson and Harris, 2019)

In some programmes, formal dissertation support groups are available to students. These may be open to all, or focused on marginalised groups, such as mature or Disabled students. In their study of two dissertation support groups for students conducting a dissertation in a foreign language, Russell-Pinson and Harris (2019) note that students were recruited from a range of disciplines (identified as broadly STEM and social sciences) at various points of their doctorates. Located within the university's counselling centre, small groups met for 1.5 hours a week for six weeks. Participants noted that the group approach allowed them to mitigate some of the stress associated with conducting their dissertation, through problem solving, relaxation techniques and goal setting. Some of the benefits were allowing students to identify signs of stress before it reached a crisis level and providing a sense of community. However, the group did also have access to specialist counsellors and referred students to other forms of support available through the university. This study shows that even those outside of your discipline may be valuable peer support buddies.

When speaking with your support buddy, you must remember to stay within the confidentiality guidelines that you have committed to in relation to your ethical approval, but it is OK to talk loosely about the contents of your data (for example, that your data showed somebody was harmed). Focus on your reaction to that and allow yourself space to process your reactions. In order to support a colleague, Box 6.5 has some examples of questions. These can also be used as prompts for your research diary.

Sketch note 6.4: Are you OK?

Box 6.5: Questions to ask your support buddy

This box is not designed to be a template to be used uncritically but may form a starting point for your peers who are finding it difficult to discuss their dissertation.

- How are you feeling about your research project?
- Is there anything that you are confused about?
- Have you started analysing your data? If not, what is the issue?
- How are you finding the content of your data? Is anything difficult to read?
- Has anything made you feel upset?

If none of that helps, please seek support from your university

If you have tried processing your thoughts alone and with a peer and you are still finding either the process of doing your research or the contents of your data distressing, seek support. The first port of call is often your supervisor. If you feel that that is inappropriate, student services at your university are likely to have support available. If these don't work, feel free to contact (probably in this order) your personal tutor, the person in charge of dissertations or your head of course/year. Please do not suffer alone. If things feel really bad, it may be time to consider seeing your doctor, or contacting a mental health organisation; in each country there are free support phone lines for mental health crisis.[1] Dissertations are hard, but they should not feel unbearable. If yours does, seek help. You have a valid reason.

Conclusion

This chapter may well have felt heavy going in relation to assessing your own position in the world and considering the emotional distress that your data can cause. If you feel uncomfortable with your **positionality**, sit with it: investigate your privilege. In this chapter we have covered the importance of understanding your **positionality** on the research process, in relation to its impact on **rigour** and your findings. The process through which you undertake an assessment of your positionality, known as **reflexivity**, can be undertaken through asking yourself questions about your demographics, views and experiences, or through a process of continuous reflection during the research process. I advocate that you continue to be **reflexive** throughout. Research diaries are often used as a tool to facilitate **reflexivity**, but they can also be used as a way of acknowledging the challenges of the research process and disturbing data. Such self-care is important and can also be achieved through supportive relationships with your peers, including nominating a specific dissertation buddy or buddies to check in with, or using avenues of formal support available from your university, doctor or mental health crisis organisations.

Further reading

Undergraduate

Barrett, A., Kajamaa, A. and Johnston, J. (2020) 'How to … be reflexive when conducting qualitative research', *The Clinical Teacher*, 17: 9–12.

Berger, R. (2015) 'Now I see it, now I don't: researcher's position and reflexivity in qualitative research', *Qualitative Research*, 15(2): 219–234.

Kara, H. (2018a) *Research Ethics in the Real World*, Bristol: Policy Press, pp 109–120.

Postgraduate

Clark, A. and Sousa, B. (2018) *How to Be a Happy Academic*, London: SAGE.

Dean, J. (2017) *Doing Reflexivity: An Introduction*, Bristol: Policy Press.

Finlay, L. (2002) 'Negotiating the swamp: the opportunity and challenge of reflexivity in research practice', *Qualitative Research*, 2: 209–230.

Kara, H. (2018a) *Research Ethics in the Real World*, Bristol: Policy Press.

Making decisions

Part II is about being curious, assembling lots of potential literature, methods and sources and thinking about how a research project could be designed. Going from a big pile of papers, methods books and potential sources to a reasonably neat and orderly **research question** and research design (sometimes called a protocol) can feel challenging. I almost called this section 'the washing machine', because of the motion that (front-loading) washing machines make; they go around and around in a clockwise direction, and then pause before going around and around in an anti-clockwise direction. The clothes – akin to your literature, data sources, analysis approaches and **research questions** – get all jumbled up during the wash. Like the washing machine cleaning the clothes within it, you too *will* get to a point where you are out the other side and have a clear idea of what body/bodies of work to discuss in your literature review, the documents that you will use as data and the analysis strategy to use; these will all clearly fit with your **research question**.

A linear approach to research design is often implied in textbooks and the reporting of research. Due to the very nature of the chapters being put into an order, this book also implies a linear structure. The purpose of Part II, however, is to highlight that this set order of 'review literature, identify question, find data' is not actually the case in real-life research using documents as data (although in the write-up of your own research this might not always be apparent, due to conventions in your department). Part II is made up of four chapters focused on the literature review, finding data, choosing an analysis strategy and finally writing **research questions** and your methods chapter. Feel free to read these in any order.

Sketch note PII.1: Don't forget to use your research diary

Figure PII.1: The cycle of developing research questions, using literature, data and analytical theory

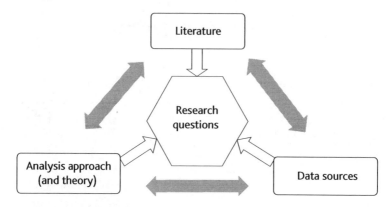

The relationship between these four topics can be viewed in Figure PII.1. The topics in the rectangles represent the first three chapters within Part II, with the dark arrows showing the cyclical relationship between the three elements. The light arrows point to the hexagon, showing that all three elements inform the **research question**. By the end of Part II, you should have identified the main elements that you need to know to write your literature review and methods chapter and to go on to begin collecting and analysing your data, which will be covered in Part III. Below, you can find more details on the contents of each chapter.

Detailed description of chapters

Chapter 7

Throughout the course of your studies, you will have learned skills in relation to reviewing evidence and crafting an argument. The literature review within your dissertation uses the same skills but requires you to take the lead in terms of searching for evidence to review. This can be a daunting task for novice and experienced researchers alike. To make the process less stressful, this chapter provides tools to help you search for literature, and to judge if the literature you find is relevant to your project. It also provides a critical appraisal framework that you can use to evaluate the quality of the articles that you are including in your review. Finally, the content and crafting of a literature review are outlined, alongside guidance on referencing and plagiarism, to ensure that your efforts in searching for and reviewing literature are fully appreciated by your examiner.

Chapter 8

You may never have had to find 'data' for a research project before, so this chapter is dedicated to making the process of finding documentary sources as logical and stress-free as possible. It may seem intimidating thinking about needing to use an **archive**, whether electronic or physical, but the skills are very similar to those you already have from using libraries to find literature (and the internet to find pictures of cute puppies – that might just be me). Once we've established that the searching itself isn't too problematic, I move on to things you should consider when deciding if sources you have found are appropriate to use for your research project. This includes whether they fit with the **research question** you would like to answer and whether it is morally and ethically appropriate to use the sources you have found within your planned research.

Chapter 9

Choosing an analysis strategy can feel like a very big decision, which is not helped by the enormous amounts of qualitative analysis strategies, and the variation in the ways that these methods are utilised, including within differing research paradigms, meaning that the methods themselves can lack specificity. That said, three major types of analysis used with documents are outlined, to make it easier for you to identify which sort of approach is most suited to your interests, **research question** and quantity of data. These approaches include **content analysis**, **thematic analysis**, **discourse analysis** and an example of using a mid-range **theory**, **Actor Network Theory**, within analysis. Following this, a consideration of integrating **theory**, piloting and **triangulation** in your study is included. Finally, the use of computer software, known as **CAQDAS** (Computer-Assisted Qualitative Data Analysis Software), to facilitate – not *do* – qualitative analysis is discussed.

Chapter 10

The final chapter within Part II brings together the information that you have gathered by working through Chapters 7, 8 and 9 in order to finalise your **research question**, which is the central component of your dissertation, on which all of the rest of the chapters hang (as can be seen in Figure PII.1). The first concept considered is how to identify a 'research gap'; I will show that this is much easier than you may think, due to literature gaps, policy changes and changes in the society under study. From here, the chapter considers what components are present in a **research question**, and how to write a good one, which is critical to achieving the top grades for your dissertation. The chapter closes by providing an outline structure for your methods chapter.

Reviewing literature and writing your literature review

Summary

This chapter will give you hints, tips and resources to ensure that you undertake high-quality scholarship in relation to your literature review. This includes ensuring that you cannot be accused of plagiarism, a serious academic offence. Also, we will consider how to identify a relevant body (or bodies) of literature, and how to critically examine it. Finally, we will consider making links between the literature that you include, to create a convincing narrative. In Part II of this book, we consider the cyclic nature of reviewing literature, choosing documents and analysis strategies to inform **research question** design. This includes acknowledging that, in practice, you may need to search for literature at several points. The overall aim is to ensure that you produce a robust, coherent and interesting literature review chapter.

Objectives

By reading this chapter, you should understand:

- where to search for literature;
- how to find *relevant* literature;
- how to refine your search if you find too much literature;
- how to critically examine your literature;
- how to structure your literature review;
- how to ensure you reference correctly, and don't inadvertently plagiarise.

Introduction: Literature reviewing can be anxiety-inducing

One area where many dissertation students feel 'stuck' is undertaking a review of relevant literature. It is not that the students are not clever, or that they lack the skills: it is that they are worried about not getting it right. Fears include missing out a single highly influential source, which would lead to embarrassment and potentially invalidate the entire project, or missing out a body of work in a related discipline. In this chapter, I hope to convey that these fears are rarely well-founded. In academia at large, there is now so much literature that it is not possible for even eminent scholars to engage in detail with all of it; therefore, we certainly would not expect undergraduate or master's students to achieve this impossible feat. Furthermore, often students will have the opportunity to have their planned literature informally assessed by their supervisor through discussions in supervision and reviewing a draft of the literature review chapter, usually at a relatively early stage. This means that any omissions that need to be addressed can be identified before the work is formally assessed. If you feel unsure or worried about what to include in your literature review, Box 7.1 provides a guide to the

Box 7.1: What is the purpose of the literature review?

Aims:

- to provide a *logical and compelling explanation* for your research;
- to provide an overview of *existing research*, and (if you are using it) **theory**;
- to bring together literature and research from multiple different areas when relevant.

Contents:

- short overview of the broader issue(s);
- more detailed consideration of research more closely related to your project;
- examination of strengths and weaknesses of the research most similar to your dissertation project;
- highlight a problem or opportunity of some sort:
  - a gap in the literature (especially in **positivist** paradigms); or
  - a change in society (this can be minor, especially within **interpretivist**, pragmatist or critical **epistemologies**); or
  - a new policy.

Structure:

- Is it logical? Does each paragraph set up the next?
- Does it lead to a single conclusion that there is value in undertaking your research project?
- The examiner marking your dissertation will be much more interested and engaged if your literature review is woven together in an interesting way.

purpose of literature review chapters, which you can return to and ask yourself whether you are responding to this requirement. You may choose to use it in line with Resource 7.3 at the end of the chapter.

How should I reference in my dissertation to avoid plagiarism?

Explaining the necessary standards this early in the chapter means that you can make sure you keep appropriately detailed references (including page numbers) as you search for literature. This serves two purposes: first, saving you time scrabbling around trying to get them at the end, and second, ensuring that you have time to get your references into the required style. Referencing consistently will make your examiner happy and inspire confidence in the authority of your work. Referencing that is error-strewn, inconsistent, sloppy or missing altogether can make your work look unprofessional, rushed, less credible and/or plagiarised. Plagiarism is a serious academic offence, which can cost you your degree. Universities are increasingly getting tough on those who plagiarise, so it is important to get your referencing right. In Box 7.2, I describe some tips to support you to avoid plagiarism.

Box 7.2: Tips on avoiding plagiarism

When finding information:

- When 'copy and pasting' into your notes, have a system so it looks different to your own writing, such as a different colour or font; AND
- keep a copy of the reference with the section (not just the name and date: use page numbers), including the URL and date for the web page and the date on which you accessed the site so that you can reference it easily; OR
- use referencing software to collect these references and insert them into your notes, if you feel that this will help you to reference consistently.

When writing draft chapters:

- Always include full referencing of the original points you include. If you include any direct quotes, use quotation marks and references, including page numbers.

Referencing

Within every part of your dissertation, wherever you draw on the ideas of somebody else, you should acknowledge this using the referencing convention

Sketch note 7.1: Don't forget to write things down

specified in your dissertation handbook. Alongside this, if you are directly quoting, you should include the page number, so the examiner can find the quote easily if required (e.g. if they think it has been taken out of context). At the end of your dissertation, you should have a full list of references.

It may seem like a quick and straightforward job to create a reference list, and many students leave this (because it's at the back of the document and not a very exciting thing to do) until last. I do not recommend this – you will be making life much harder for yourself if you do not compile the list (or at least gather the information you need to create it) as you go along. You need to make sure you only have reference details for sources that you cite in the text; other sources should be excluded unless specified in your dissertation guide. Resource 7.1 provides a list of tips for ensuring that your referencing is correct, with actions undertaken throughout your dissertation process.

Should I use referencing software?

There are many types of referencing software, some free and others requiring a licence. When writing your dissertation, it is not unusual for you to read a few hundred items and cite around a hundred items. You may manage these by collating a list of everything you've read within a word processing program, a specific notebook or on summary sheets that you create for each item you have read. If you plan to keep handwritten notes on paper, I recommend regularly taking photos or scans of your written work. Low-tech ways of gathering information may be preferable if learning how to use a new referencing program does not feel like a good use of your time, particularly for undergraduates.

If you do use referencing software, remember that the bibliography created is only as good as the information it retrieves – this may include things like not downloading full citation details, including an essential part of the reference (such as

Resource 7.1: Referencing checklist

To do	Tick	Notes
Find out what style of referencing you are required to use.		
Ensure you understand how to use this type of referencing.		
If you decide to use referencing software, get familiar with how to use it. *This can take a while.*		
As you are reading, keep records of the literature you are reviewing.		
As you are writing, reference every source that you have used in the text at the appropriate place(s). *Do this as you go along so that you do not plagiarise by mistake.*		
Each time you make changes to your literature review, save it as a new version. *If you delete a section by mistake, you can easily find it again.*		
Create a reference list as you go along.		

the date, or the volume number of the journal), using all capital letters sometimes, and getting information wrong, such as spelling mistakes and missing **authors**.

Where should I search for literature?

Box 7.3 provides a stepped approach to help prioritise reading within your undergraduate dissertation project; master's and doctoral students should consider starting with supervisor recommendations and your own searching. If you feel overwhelmed by the freedom afforded, try not to panic. My advice is to think back to your plan (see Chapter 3): how much time do you have available to do your literature review? Try not to go over the time 'budget' you have set yourself as you follow the steps in Box 7.3.

> ### Box 7.3: Checklist: how to choose literature – a stepped approach
>
> - Review old reading lists and notes on the topic.
>   - ◦ Read literature that is cited by papers on your reading list; also search for papers that cite particularly relevant papers.
> - Speak to your supervisor and ask for recommendations.
> - Search for literature yourself.
> - Don't panic if your search terms provide an overwhelming number of results.
> - Make your search terms more specific, until you find a reasonable number of articles to review.
> - If you have literature on two or three different topics that need to be included, try to balance the number of papers for each topic if there is good quality evidence on each topic.
> - Start drafting the structure for your literature review (see Resource 7.3).
> - Select the papers with the strongest evidence for each part of your literature review.

So, where should you start? If you have studied this area previously, refresh your knowledge by skimming the books and articles on your reading lists. Likewise, if you have been assigned a supervisor, they can usually signpost you to relevant literature (make sure you note this down). Once you have exhausted these two areas, it's time to search an academic database. There are a range of databases, containing journal articles, book chapters and even dissertations. Each database covers a particular area of study, so within your discipline there are likely to be one or two key databases. For example, within public health research, MedLine and Web of Science (which also includes the Arts & Humanities Citation Index) are the two most common. Most of these databases require a licence, which will be held by your university. If

Sketch note 7.2: Read widely

you are unsure how to access them, your university's intranet or librarians should be able to help you. Even if you haven't searched an academic database before, if you can search the internet, you are well equipped to do this task.

How do I search for literature on my topic?

In this section, you will be taken through the basics of searching for literature, i.e. what to actually include in the search bar of the database you are going to

Sketch note 7.3: Databases are your friends

Sketch note 7.4: Record information *as you search*

use. First, you need to be clear about what you are searching for, so that you do not get distracted by interesting literature that is only tangentially linked to your topic. I will describe how to use **Boolean operators**, such as AND and NOT, which help you to narrow down the results that you find from databases.

Search terms are very important

I approach literature reviewing imagining it as funnel shaped *or* a series of unrelated sections. With the funnel approach, you start with the big picture to set the scene. You then get narrower and more detailed as you progress, leading the **reader**, inevitably, to the conclusion that your **research question** is important and needs to be answered. You include less of the general literature and more detail in relation to the more narrowly focused literature as you go on. Finding the right words to describe the narrow area that you are interested in is key to identifying the most relevant literature. It is not always possible to fit your literature into a single stream, and this approach is known as stacking boxes; you introduce two or more broad concepts and bring them together at the end of the literature review through a concluding paragraph. Regardless, the literature you really want to find is that which is most related to the narrow topic you are interested in. Box 7.4 provides some ideas to help you find your keywords.

Boolean operators

Boolean operators, such as AND and OR, can be used to help you narrow down the literature that you are looking for. Table 7.1 includes common **Boolean operators** and their functions within academic database searches, using an example of combining two topics (sport and fruit). Box 7.5 is a more detailed example of how and why I amended a search strategy using **Boolean operators** to achieve a usable **sample** size, in a project relating to infant feeding and Autism.

Above I described how to narrow the focus of your literature search. But what if you have the opposite problem? If you are returning too few articles, you need to think about how you could expand your search. Box 7.6 is an example of how you could expand your search if you were reviewing literature in relation to cheating in dog competitions. This example is fictitious, but surprisingly when I did a Google Scholar search, I returned only 118 articles and very few appeared relevant; this could be a topic in need of research (or probably a more thorough literature search).

> **Box 7.4: Inspiration for your search terms**
>
> - Think of the people or objects (often a noun) that you are interested in; people from a particular place, uniforms, diaries, etc.
> - Use a dictionary or thesaurus to find alternative terms for the same central object.
> - Snowballing: when you find one relevant paper, look at the **keywords** (usually found below the **abstract**) and see if any look suitable to use as a search term.

Table 7.1: Using common Boolean operators: an example based on sport and fruit

Operator	Function: search results...	Example
AND	Must include both words	Sport AND fruit
OR	Can include multiple variations of the concept, including synonyms	Sport AND orange OR lemon
NOT	Must not include a specific term	Sport AND fruit NOT tomato
'...'	Must have that specific term, with the words in that order	Sport AND 'passion fruit'
()	Prioritise that part of the search – this is important for long searches with more than one **Boolean operator**	Sport AND (fruit OR orange OR lemon)

How do I know if the literature I've found is relevant?

As long as you are clear about what is important to your dissertation topic, you can assess the papers against that. You may not be at this stage yet, and I advise you to be curious and pursue areas that you find interesting or unusual. Keeping notes will help you to make links between interesting but seemingly unrelated articles as you proceed through your literature searches.

The number of sources included in the literature chapter will vary by a range of factors, including the length of your dissertation, the amount of relevant literature, how important and/or detailed the 'interrogation' of core papers is, and any departmental requirements. I suggest referring to your notes on project planning and the marking scheme, including what your examiners are looking for. Often, to achieve higher grades, an analytic and critical review of the literature is required.

When should I stop searching for more literature?

Often, students worry about a (nearly always fictional) really important single paper that would completely change their dissertation. If your supervisor is happy that your literature review is sufficient, stop searching databases. However, it is good practice to ensure that you are citing a diverse (i.e. female, Disabled, Black

Sketch note 7.5: Be methodical and organised

Box 7.5: Narrowing the focus of your literature search using Boolean operators: an example of breastfeeding and Autistic women

I undertook a search for views and experiences of breastfeeding and Autistic women. I searched initially using the funnel approach that I would use to structure a six-paragraph literature review (described in Sketch note 7.7). This means that you start broad, and get narrower and narrower until you get a usable number of hits. These were the results I got:

Search 1: Breastfeeding – 804,000

This was far too broad – I could not have looked at even the abstracts of these papers in the time I had.

Search 2: Breastfeeding AND Autism – 16,000

Skimming the abstracts of these articles, most were about a possible association (it would not be ethical to carry out experiments to test causation – see Brown (2019)) between formula feeding and Autism in children, which is not the purpose of my study. As such, this search can also be disregarded.

Search 3: Breastfeeding AND 'Autistic women' – 26 results

As there were so few abstracts, I was able to read them all fully. There were a few papers that were obviously central to my literature review. If you are researching a topic where there is limited literature, you may need to search through papers where your topic is not the central focus to pick out the small nuggets of knowledge on your topic area.

Box 7.6: Expanding your literature search

If your dissertation was focused on cheating within elite dog competitions, and you had tried lots of variations of words for all three elements ('cheating' AND 'dog' AND 'competition') but returned few papers, it would be time to expand your search terms. Think about which of the three elements you would like to expand first (i.e. keep two of the terms the same and expand one).

I would imagine that cheating and elite competitions are the important bits of this dissertation (they may not be), so would then expand my search by considering other animals used in elite sports, such as horses and pigeons. If that did not return sufficient results, I could move on to consider either expanding out from elite only competitions OR removing the concept 'cheating' from my search, instead considering qualitative literature and grey literature/documentaries on what happens at dog competitions, to uncover potentially unfair practices.

and Indigenous) range of scholars to reduce structural inequality within academia. I suggest some ways to move beyond the mainstream in Box 7.8.

If you draft your literature review and it feels well rounded, you are ready to stop searching, subject to your supervisor's agreement. You may also be running out of time. Remember that a perfect literature review alone cannot get you a good grade if you are doing a research-based dissertation: you will need to do the research and write it up too.

Box 7.7: How to read a paper to assess relevance

It is absolutely not necessary to read every paper in full.

That's important, so I'll say it again: it is not necessary to read a paper in full to decide whether it is relevant.

Start by reading the abstract. If it appears relevant, a useful way to approach speed-reading a paper is to look at the headings throughout and read the conclusion. At this point, you should have an idea as to which parts of the article you can briefly skim, and the parts that you need to read in detail, simultaneously identifying, and perhaps extracting, core information to decide if that paper is important enough to help shape your study, and/or if it belongs in your literature review chapter.

How do I critically examine the literature in my literature review?

Once you have found all your literature, the first step is to read the papers, and make notes highlighting the findings that relate to your planned research topic or draft **research question**, as well as the quality of the methodology and the **sample** of data that was used. You may wish to use Resource 7.2 to help you take notes, or you may choose to make notes on the paper, in your research diary, or anywhere else that feels right to you. When you review a paper fully, you may identify **biases** in the methodology. If these are serious, you may wish to mention that research only in passing in your literature review and include another, methodologically stronger paper from your search, if there is a suitable alternative.

Box 7.8: Tips to help find diverse literature

- Make a note of first names as well as last names when collecting references; this will often help you to identify the gender of the researcher.
- Within journal articles, the **authors'** institution is usually listed. Search for them online to see how diverse your scholars are from their institutional web pages.
- Ask your supervisor for guidance on who the critical scholars are in your field.
- Identify charities, think tanks and organisations who have an opinion on your topic and search for reports they have produced.

Sketch note 7.6: Go on ... draft a structure: it's OK to change it later

A core skill within dissertations, as within many social science and humanities essays, is to craft an argument. This shows that you have read and understood the literature, that you understand its strengths and weaknesses, and that you can situate it within the context of other relevant material. To do so, you need to bring together the key points from the literature: for example, categorising the findings into positives/negatives, barriers/facilitators, views of Group A/ views of Group B, historical trends, etc. You may also want to directly compare the methodologies of different pieces of research with their results. If you are struggling to identify a useful way of bringing together your literature, I suggest examining good examples of dissertations in your university library for the way they presented their literature review and considering what the point of each paragraph was. Finally, draw a conclusion relating to the strength and quality of the research available, providing either your **research question** or a statement that research is needed on this topic. Some disciplines place their **research question** at the end of the literature review, while others place it at the beginning of the methods chapter. Ensure you follow the conventions within your department.

How should I structure my literature review?

I recommend discussing expectations for the structure of your chapter with your supervisor, and/or examining dissertations from previous students to see how to structure your literature review chapter for success *in your department*. Alongside this, I recommend the 'funnel' approach to structuring a dissertation – starting with the broadest information and getting more specific the further you progress, as shown in Sketch note 7.7. If you use the 'stacked boxes' approach to structuring your literature review, each of the 'boxes' of separate literature can be a funnel in itself.

A suggested structure for your literature review, following the funnel approach, can be found in Resource 7.3. This may seem too abstract for some **readers**, so in Box 7.9 I return to the search that I undertook earlier on breastfeeding and Autism (see Box 7.6). These key terms can be used to help structure the literature review.

Resource 7.2: Critically reviewing a journal article

Reference:

Overview

Literature to look up

Methods (data, analysis type)

Data (quality, quantity and appropriateness)

Main results

Conclusions

Resource 7.3: Structuring your literature review

Section	Paragraph details/ purpose	Planned word count	Details								
Introduction (1 paragraph)											
Big picture information											
More detailed information about your topic(s)											
Detailed analysis of the data, analysis and findings of the most similar research											
Research question											
Conclusion (1 paragraph)											

Sketch note 7.7: The funnel approach to literature reviewing

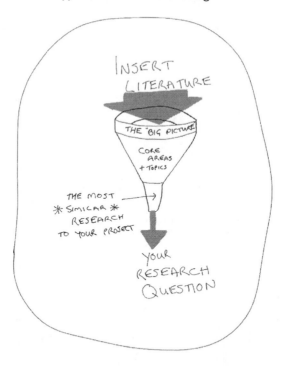

Box 7.9: An example of structuring the literature review: Autistic women's experiences of breastfeeding

Paragraph 1: give some introductory information in relation to breastfeeding – recommended practice compared to breastfeeding rates. Separately I would give key information on Autism, such as definitions and prevalence.

Paragraph 2: describe the key papers found relating to Autism and breastfeeding in contemporary research – these mostly relate to the correlation (which does not mean there is a cause) between breastfeeding mothers and lower prevalence of Autistic children.

Paragraphs 3–6: detail on the views and experiences of breastfeeding Autistic women. Perhaps structured as barriers to breastfeeding (paragraph 3), facilitators to breastfeeding (paragraph 4), variation in barriers and facilitators compared to neurotypical women (paragraph 5), which leads to the **research question** and conclusion (paragraph 6).

Conclusion

This chapter has taken you through the process of undertaking a literature review for your dissertation. There are many potential pitfalls in this area of your dissertation, as it is a potentially infinite piece of work. However, I have provided some guidelines and tools that will hopefully enable you to complete your literature review within the time you have allowed and as required in your marking scheme. I have also described how poor referencing can potentially lead to you failing your dissertation due to plagiarism allegations. In the next chapter, we move on to considering finding sources to use as data, the second of the three factors that will influence your **research question** and design.

Further reading

Undergraduate

Bell, J. and Waters, S. (2014) *Doing Your Research Project: A Guide for First-time Researchers*, New York: Open University Press, pp 87–103 and pp 104–118.
Galvan, J.L. and Galvan, M.C. (2017) *Writing Literature Reviews: A Guide for Students of the Social and Behavioural Sciences*, Abingdon: Routledge.

Postgraduate

Hart, C. (2018) *Doing a Literature Review: Releasing the Research Imagination*, London: SAGE.
Ridley, D. (2012) *The Literature Review: A Step-by-step Guide for Students*, London: SAGE.

8

Finding sources

Summary

This chapter takes you through a range of questions to help you choose your sources purposefully. First, we look at when to start looking for sources (now – there's no harm in 'window shopping', but remember to take notes). We then think about aligning your topic or **research question** with the sources you are considering. After this, we consider where to find documents, both in formal **archives** and from the internet. Finally, we consider if the sources you have in mind are ethically appropriate.

Objectives

By reading this chapter, you should understand:

- when you should start searching for documents;
- what sort of sources will answer your **research question**;
- how to identify documents within **archives**;
- where to identify documentary sources online;
- why sources may be appropriate or inappropriate.

Introduction: Documents come from EVERYWHERE!

Sometimes a data source jumps out at me and I think that I simply must write about those data in relation to some literature or a **theory** I already know about. One example is my research with Hannah O'Mahoney (Grant and O'Mahoney, 2016) where we looked at content on Twitter relating to waterpipe smoking. Prior to starting the application for funding, I had noticed that a lot of businesses were promoting shisha nights in a glamorous way that is no longer seen in relation to cigarette smoking, due to legal restrictions. At other times, I start thinking about a type of data and wondering if anybody has done any research on that particular thing. This happened to me in relation to 'baby product awards' where magazines rate new baby gadgets; I wondered who the vested interests were and the sorts of language used in the write-ups, to see if it was emotive, classist, or if it broke the law in relation to undermining breastfeeding. These two examples illustrate that there is not a single 'right' or 'wrong' way to find your documents. Sometimes you may find documents and get excited about them, and then realise they aren't quite right; that's OK too.

When should I start searching for documents?

There is no fixed answer to this question, unfortunately, depending on the way that you are being guided to undertake your project! In general, I – someone who is not at all laid back – would choose to start looking as soon as possible. This doesn't have to be extensive, but before doing a full literature review, it is sensible to assess if there are sufficient data for you to analyse in relation to that topic. That's why I have structured the book in parts: this middle *Making decisions* section where you are required to be curious has to be navigated together to some extent. One key factor in deciding when to start your search is how challenging you think it is likely to be to access potential sources of data. If you plan to analyse data that are in the public domain, and likely to remain in the public domain long-term, such as policy or (social) media documents, it is absolutely fine to begin collecting documents close to when you have a full draft of your literature review, as you know that there will be some data. However, if you are less clear about the sources that you intend to include in your analysis, such as if you plan to use historical data, it is sensible to secure access to your data before writing your literature review.

Sketch note 8.1: Be curious

As noted above, I have begun several research projects because something I read inspired me to take a deeper, more critical look. I knew I needed to do some research on these documents because I kept thinking about them, talking to others about them, and linking parts of the documents' contents to my social science knowledge. If you are at this stage, remember, it's OK (and still scientific) to design a research project in a 'data first' way. However, the way you write up your dissertation – or any other type of research report – is nearly always that you talk about the literature and then introduce the documents.

What sort of sources will answer my research question?

This is a very, very important question and one of the hardest to answer. I strongly recommend that you discuss this with your supervisor. If your **research question** has to be written a certain way, or is fixed because of another factor, it is very important that your data fit the **research question**. This will definitely be assessed by your examiner (if you find yourself with a rigid **research question**, please skip ahead to Chapter 10 and then return to this chapter). Once you have a **research question** formatted in line with the conventions of your department, you can see if your data are suitable. You may wish to consider the elements in Box 8.1 to decide if the data are adequate in relation to period, topic, **theory**, quantity and depth.

Box 8.1: Matching potential sources to research questions

Consider if your sources could be used to answer your **research question** in relation to:

- The historical period
  - If not, does this matter?
- The broad topic
  - If not, is it close enough? Or could the question be amended?
- Any theoretical perspective you are using
  - If not, do any other theories seem relevant if you require a theoretical perspective?
- The quantity of data
  - If not, could you supplement, or triangulate, the data with other sources?
- The 'richness' of detail related to your particular **research question**
  - Again, if not, could you supplement or triangulate?

Sometimes it is very straightforward to recognise the types of sources that you wish to include, and the narrowing down occurs in relation to sub-classifications, as can be seen within an exemplar dissertation from the Leeds University Business School, UK (200614195, 2014), presented in Box 8.2.

An example to illustrate how to find sources for more difficult-to-identify topics (due to their relative breadth) is in Box 8.3. The example is based on a historical project using school magazines to consider 'citizenship' during a historical period. If your research is based on a concept that, for example, was not familiar during the context (time, location, etc.) of data production or was described with different language, you may need to search for hidden clues in other sources. I provide more detailed examples elsewhere (see Grant, 2021).

Box 8.2: Student example: using newspapers as sources, but which newspapers? (200614195, 2014)

Within a dissertation focused on the representation of women in business, the student, referred to anonymously by their student number alone (200614195, 2014), focused on newspaper content related to businesswomen. However, it is never as simple as saying your sources are 'newspapers': they need to be confined by location, publication and period. Situated within a social constructionist **epistemology**, the student decided on the following boundaries data (p 13):

- Where: UK and USA, allowing comparative analysis between the countries.
- Publication: large national newspapers; *The Times* and *The New York Times*.
- Period of time: March 2013, to include International Women's Day.
- Topic: narrowed to be manageable within a dissertation through the use of a 'search string' (reported within Appendix 1 of the dissertation).

Sketch note 8.2: Keep notes as you search

Box 8.3: Finding hidden sources to explore citizenship in the past

In her research on citizenship in the Interwar Period (between the First and Second World Wars, 1919–1939), Susannah Wright (2020) took the novel approach of considering an inter-country education initiative targeted at children. In order to explore the area in sufficient detail to draw conclusions, she examined school magazines from four schools teaching pupils aged around 7–11 years of age. In so doing, Wright argues that it was possible to understand the culture of the four schools included, and therefore to say something significant about their approach to citizenship. In particular, this analysis allowed for conclusions relating to the educational initiatives' ideals and policies, and how their impacts on citizenship were used (or not), altered and promoted.

Where to search for documents

This section will consider three locations: **archives**, private data not held in an archive, and material available on the internet. Box 8.4 describes some ways of identifying documents that may be useful and highlights the non–linear approach that is commonly used in this period of developing a research design.

Archives

Archives are formal repositories containing documents and artefacts, such as maps, letters, wills, photographs and records from local government, often from historical periods. What is stored in an **archive** is decided by those who fund archives and **archivists** who process and catalogue sources, and is thus not a

Box 8.4: Ways of identifying documentary sources

- Something you already know about that has made a strong impression on you.
- When you are discussing an area of interest, somebody tells you about some relevant documentary sources.
- You have an area of interest, and you actively look for sources of data within this area which will help you refine your **research questions**.
- You have a **research question**, and you actively look for sources of data to help you answer that specific question.

neutral reporting of history. There has been an increasing move in recent years, however, to create more inclusive citizen archives, including within existing archives (e.g. The National Archives (UK)), and through hyperlocal journalism (Blaggard, 2019). Archives can be both physical buildings, akin to libraries, and/ or online archives. Documents within physical **archives** will often need to be reviewed on site or you may have the opportunity to make your own copies. It can be helpful to have a work plan in place prior to attending the **archive** to make the most of your visit and avoid feeling overwhelmed. Questions include: are you going to try to make a copy of the data (is that allowed?) or analyse your data on site? What do you need to take with you? For the purposes of your dissertation, which is of course time-limited, it may be easier to focus on online **archives**. If you plan to collect data in person, see Moore et al (2017) for details on successful archival research, including what it might be helpful to take with you.

Most countries have a national **archive**, including The National Archives Administration of China, the National Library of South Africa, The National Archives of India and The German National Archive. The website of The National Archives (UK), is a fantastic resource, which contains a guide on how to use **archives** if this is new to you and an A–Z guide to topics and historical periods. Once you have registered for a free account, you can download digital sources for free. As well as this, The National Archives website contains a list of UK and international **archives**. If you are an undergraduate who does not know where to start searching for a source, I would highly recommend that you begin with the National Archive in the country you plan to study.

Sketch note 8.3: Don't forget to be ethical

Finding sources on the internet

There is a huge variety of documentary data available on the internet. Sources include those aimed at the general public, including those provided by organisations such as governments and businesses, and those created by individuals such as **blogs** and social media content. Box 8.5 provides an example of one way of searching for media content, using the **Nexis®** database. Other online content tends to be searched using regular internet search engines. Because of the interactive nature of the internet, much social media content is intended to only be viewed by those with the shared specialist interest. This content may be contained, for example, on a forum or a sub-group on a social media platform, such as Facebook groups and Reddit subs.

Whether content in these spaces can be viewed as appropriate, or 'fair game', to be used as data in a research project is contentious. It has previously been stated that no ethical approval is required for content in the public domain (see, for example, Mann and Stewart, 2000); this has affected several of my studies undertaken at Cardiff University. These days, some content creators are more savvy, including statements asserting that they *do not* give permission for their content to be used elsewhere, and researchers are more critical of routinely allowing such content to be used as data. I suggest you consult the AoIR's code of ethical guidance (franzke et al, 2020) and discuss the matter with your supervisor to ensure good ethical practice.

Box 8.5: Searching for media accounts of using donor breast milk using the Nexis® database

If mums choose not to breastfeed their babies, or are unable to, the World Health Organization says that they should be given donor milk from another mother. This is relatively rare these days in the global North. To find out how it is portrayed within the media, Sally Dowling and I (Dowling and Grant, 2021) decided to find newspaper articles from around the world. The **Nexis®** database is often available within academic institutions. It can be searched just like the databases that contain literature, including using **Boolean operators**. We included a list of potential words describing breast milk, and another describing donors. Over a two-year period, we found over 100 media documents, mostly from newspapers in America, Australia and the UK. Using **Nexis®** allowed us to search an enormous number of publications for relevant content very quickly. If you do not have access to **Nexis®**, you could search the individual websites of relevant media sources, although this would take longer.

Sketch note 8.4: Letters are an exciting form of data

Finding hard copies of data

It is true that some archival content is hard copies of data, particularly from historical periods prior to the advent of the internet. However, that is not the only kind of hard copy that can be used as data. Hard copy sources include those in the public domain, such as magazines, leaflets and posters, and those not publicly available, such as family photographs, diaries and letters.

Publicly available data can provide a window into popular culture and consumption habits in capitalist societies. A wide range of research has been undertaken in relation to the packaging and advertising of products. For instance, an entire online archive, the *Truth Tobacco Industry Documents*, and peer-reviewed academic journal *Tobacco Control*, are now dedicated to examining the marketing of tobacco products, including cigarette packaging, advertising in various forms and point-of-sale displays in shops. These data are often interesting in content (see, for example, the advertising campaign focusing on animals' bottoms: Harty, 1993). Marketing materials can also be easily collected by students, by taking photos and collecting documents, making it a popular choice for dissertations.

Using personal documents, by contrast, usually occurs because of a connection between the holder of the documents and the researcher (or perhaps their supervisor), and these sources can be much trickier to access. For example, a friend offered me access to documents from the Second World War that she found in her grandfather's home after he had died. Local historical societies may also have access to documents of interest, and some publish books of photographs and other documents. If original documents are offered, extreme care must be taken with them, so that they are not lost or damaged in any way. Researchers using personal documents must also ensure that informed consent is gained from the holder of the documents, and that there is a clear agreement about how the documents will be used. Remember, the holder of the documents can decide to withdraw their consent and leave you without any data if they are unhappy with your research, so it is important to be very clear about expectations. Because of the sharing of personal information, it is likely that a project using documents from a personal contact would need ethical approval and for you to record the owner's consent.

How to search for sources in archives

If you feel confident searching for literature within academic databases (see Chapter 7, especially the section on **Boolean operators**), you already have the skills to search for sources in online **archives**. There are three main things that you need to consider in your searches: the time, theme and type of sources. These are noted in Box 8.6 as a prompt. *How* to use these three concepts is generally the same as any online search, with one small exception. If you are not investigating a defined historical period (e.g. Victorian), you can restrict items by time, through the use of start and end dates, which are usually separate from, and below, the main search bar.

Table 8.1 shows a worked example of designing a search using these three questions, focused on a fictitious research project into historical dental care in the UK. You may choose to replicate this table in your own research, adding any extra criteria relevant to your own project. Below I go on to examine the three questions in Box 8.6 in relation to this example search for documents.

Box 8.6: Concepts to include in searches for sources

Your search could include:

1. the period of time that you are interested in;
2. the theme that you wish to explore;
3. the type of sources that you wish to find, and any that you definitely do not want to.

Table 8.1: Finding documents on dental care in the UK from 1940 to 1970

Search criteria	Response
The period of time that you are interested in	1940–1970
The theme that you wish to explore	Dental care in the UK
The type of sources that you are interested in consulting, including any that you will not include	Interested in: any records that shed light on the teeth of marginalised groups, oral care and access to dentistry

Table 8.2: Identifying alternative terms to search for sources on your topic of interest

Search strategy	Example relating to dentistry 1940–1970
Use alternative words	Instead of dental, we could use teeth, oral health, dentures
Use a broader topic area	Instead of dental, we could think of health
Use your knowledge of the topic area to think of specialist terms. If you cannot think of any, you can search 'key words'[1] of journal articles based around your topic.	Significant change occurred in 1948 with the introduction of the NHS. As such, I could search for the National Health Service, National Dental Service and professional bodies that represented dentists.

Note: [1] 'Keywords' tend to be found below the abstract in journal articles and are based on the core topics of that article.

Narrowing your period of interest

When the UK National Health Service was introduced in 1948, dental care became free to all UK residents at the point of use. This was because the poor state of the nation's teeth had become apparent at the end of the previous century during the Boer War. Because of this knowledge, I am able to narrow down my period of interest. If you are returning too many sources, you could narrow your time period if it is methodologically justifiable.

Developing search terms

I was fortunate in my example that by searching for 'dental', I was able to find relevant content. Sometimes this is not the case, and it can be tricky to find sources. Some ways to expand your key words can be found in Table 8.2.

Identifying the type of sources of interest

Within the term 'marginalised groups' in Table 8.1, I considered those who were on the fringes of society, including the poor, unemployed, Disabled and immigrants, so I could have used these words to narrow my search if I was overwhelmed with too many results. When I used this strategy within The National Archives website, I found a range of hard copy and online data; you can find more detail in Box 8.7.

Very occasionally, it can feel impossible to find any relevant sources. If this happens, see Box 8.8 for guidance on broadening the topic you are searching for.

Box 8.7: Searching The National Archives website for NHS and dentistry

A selection of the immediate results included:

- *Barking and Dagenham Archives and Local Studies Centre* have records on the 'Welfare of the Blind: minutes, corresp [sic] and annual reports 1936–1992'.
- *Bath and North-East Somerset Record Office* have a collection of notes from a geriatrician, Michael Rowe.

Using one of these **archives**, I could examine documents in relation to Blind people and dental health during the 1930s–90s, or the notes of a medical doctor who specialises in the care of older people, who may have had a greater requirement for dental care. The results of my study would almost certainly vary depending on which source I used.

If I did not have the time to go to a local **archive** in person, I would change my search term to only include 'national' **archives**, most of which have at least part of their collection online. Doing this, I can see that *The Wellcome Collection*, a UK medical **archive**, is included and there are many sources available when I search for 'dental'. Furthermore, *The Wellcome Collection* **archive** allows me to choose a range of dates, so I can narrow my search. This leaves me with 22 sources related to dental care, which feels like it could be a large enough **sample** for a project.

Box 8.8: Help! I can't find any relevant sources in the archive

When this happens, it can leave even experienced researchers feeling terrified. If this happens to you, it is completely OK to have a moment of panic. Then it is time to:

- Try using all the potential search terms for your topic with *only* the time period selected.
- Expand your search terms into a broader topic area (as in Table 8.2).
- Think about *why* you are struggling to find data; what was the political and social context at the time? Might there be alternative keywords?
- Take a break and come back to this tomorrow.
- If you are still struggling, send your supervisor a list of the searches you have run and ask for help in considering other potential search terms.

Conclusion

This chapter has guided you through the core areas of identifying documents to use as data for your dissertation from official **archives**, hard copy data and the internet. The core points to remember as you choose your own data are: sources need to be suitable to answer your **research question**, that is, they contain enough information on the specific narrow topic that you are studying; and that the data should be appropriate from an ethical point of view, so that you cannot be accused of exploiting the **authors**. Once you have chosen your **research question** and data, the big decisions for your dissertation have been made, so – if at all possible – take some time to get this right.

Further reading

Undergraduate

Brundage, A. (2018) *Going to the Sources: A Guide to Historical Research and Writing* (6th edn), London: Wiley Blackwell, pp 30–50.

Claus, P. and Marriott, J. (2012) *History: An Introduction to Theory, Method and Practice*, Abingdon: Routledge, pp 365–404.

Largan, C. and Morris, T. (2019) *Qualitative Secondary Research: A Step-by-step Guide*, London: SAGE, pp 144–164.

Postgraduate

Buss, H.M. and Kadar, M. (2001) *Working in Women's Archives: Researching Women's Private Literature and Archival Documents*, Waterloo, Ontario: Wilfrid Laurier University Press.

Prior, L. (2003) *Using Documents in Social Research*, London: SAGE.

Choosing an analysis approach

Summary

If doing analysis is new to you, don't worry: we will consider a range of commonly used qualitative analysis types in this chapter. This includes **content analysis, thematic analysis, discourse analysis** and **Actor Network Theory**. For each type of analysis, I provide a description and an approach to undertaking the analysis, and make comments on the sorts of **sample** size that may be appropriate. Following this, the chapter considers the use of **theory** alongside your analysis strategy, triangulation, and the use of computer software, known as **CAQDAS** to facilitate (not *do*) your analysis. Remember, you are still in the 'making decisions stage', and all of the chapters in Part II are things to consider together. In Chapter 11, which focuses on what to do once you have your data, the practice of coding data, which is at the heart of qualitative analysis, will be considered.

Objectives

By reading this chapter, you should understand:

- the differences between some core types of analysis strategies;
- why you might choose to use **theory** within your analysis (or not);
- how to do **triangulation** within documentary analysis;
- why you might choose to use qualitative analysis software during your analysis (or not).

Introduction: The importance of choosing an analysis approach *before* your data

It is really important that you understand that the amount and type of data you need varies *hugely* between analysis strategies. For example, I analysed thousands of social media posts in one project. By contrast, during my undergraduate years, a fantastic social policy lecturer, Paul Lodge, spent around 15 hours of lectures taking us through a single speech delivered by

Tony Blair, then Prime Minister of the UK, which was less than two sides of A4 long. We interrogated it as thoroughly as possible, using something akin to **discourse analysis**, but associated with a detailed knowledge and application of historical social policy. To choose a form of analysis, think about your ontological and epistemological position (see Chapter 2) and the impact this has on your research paradigm and methodology. Positivistic approaches tend not to interrogate data in depth, whereas **interpretivist**, pragmatist and other non-**positivist** approaches consider **meaning** and context as part of analysis in various ways. Approaches such as **content analysis** and **thematic analysis** can be used in ways that are more positivistic, such as the use of pre-defined (**deductive**) codes, or more interpretivistic, such as the use of **inductive** codes.

How can I fit my analysis strategy within my research paradigm?

Traditional approaches to undertaking documentary analysis are situated within positivistic research paradigms and focus on a relatively superficial and uncritical consideration of the contents (both written and graphical) of documents (Prior, 2003). One of the most common approaches within this tradition is **content analysis**, although this has been built on in recent years by qualitative **content analysis**, which is more interpretative in nature. Traditional **content analysis** is the quickest and often easiest way to analyse a small **sample** of documentary sources, because it reports on the content uncritically. As **content analysis** is situated within positivistic traditions, it is common for larger **sample**s of data to be used, as a single universal 'truth' is sought. Emphasis may also be placed on how replicable the analysis is.

We can learn more from documents by using interpretivistic approaches to 'read between the lines' and search for deeper **meaning** in either the documents' content or function. **Discourse analysis** is a strategy based in an ethnomethodological paradigm, in which researchers consider language and **meaning** in great detail. **Reflexive Thematic Analysis** (Braun and Clarke, 2020) is another approach focused on identifying views and experiences of phenomena, which is unashamedly situated within a context where researcher **positionality** influences the 'themes', which in turn impact on the findings.

There are no fixed definitions of **content**, **discourse** or **thematic analysis**. I recommend finding a methodological text that guides you through the type of analysis you wish to do (I suggest some later in the chapter) and following those steps precisely. The analysis strategy you choose can impact the quantity of data that you need to include in your analysis, with positivistic approaches to analysis generally requiring larger data sets. Below I provide more detail about each of these approaches. A detailed worked example of each of these analysis approaches can be found in my first book (Grant, 2019) – **content analysis** in Chapter 5, **thematic analysis** in Chapter 3, and **discourse analysis** in Chapter 4.

Sketch note 9.1: Follow a respected analysis guide

What is content analysis and how do I decide which things to count?

At the most positivistic end of documentary analysis lie traditional approaches to **content analysis**. Like many of the analysis strategies discussed, there is no single definition of **content analysis**, and so researchers must rely on choosing one type, and follow those guidelines. If this does not seem appropriate, we can mix elements from more than one type, but we will need to defend why that was decided. One interpretation of **content analysis** is outlined in Table 9.1. I have drawn my interpretation of **content analysis** from my reading of a large number of sources, but primarily use definitions and processes from Schreier (2014). This is explored in further detail below.

The common factor within **content analysis** strategies is to devise a coding framework, and then rigorously and systematically apply it to all the data within the research project. In practice, this means that researchers decide on the things they want to find within the data and make a list, called the coding framework. To make sure that the **content analysis** is high quality, each small segment within the data is checked for the presence of every code. You may sometimes hear this approach referred to as line-by-line coding. The unique factor in many forms of **content analysis** compared to other analysis strategies is that the **coding framework** is developed during a **piloting** phase, and new codes cannot be added after it is finalised. Two elements apply within **content analysis** that are specifically designed to fit within a **positivist** tradition: **piloting** and **double coding**. **Piloting** is used to make sure that no new codes are needed, that is, that the coding framework accurately describes all aspects of the data that can contribute to answering the **research question**; this is something that an **interpretivist** would view as impossible. Some forms of **content analysis** strongly recommend that, in order to test for construct **validity**, at least some of the data should be independently coded by a second researcher, and any inconsistencies noted and

Table 9.1: Steps in content analysis (Schreier, 2014)

Step	My notes
Develop coding framework	This can be based on reviewing the data, existing topics of interest, or even specific people, things or events.
Generate definitions for codes	Sometimes known as creating a 'coding book' or 'coding log', the function of this is to be as clear as possible about what a code includes and excludes, so that in theory somebody else could *exactly* replicate your findings if they used your codes and data.
Decide on size of data extracts	This means splitting your data into segments which are broadly equal, e.g. a segment is equal to one tweet, but larger pieces of text may need to be considered one sentence at a time.
Piloting	Test your coding framework on a range of documents.
Refine and finalise coding	Update your coding framework if needed after the piloting. It should then be 'locked' with no further changes allowed.
Code the whole data set	Use the coding framework only.
Consider **meanings**	This can include latent and symbolic as well as explicit **meanings**.
Double coding	The analysis, or a proportion of it, from the 'code the whole data set' step forward, should be repeated by a second person. Differences in coding should be calculated (sometimes using statistical tests) and resolved.

discussed so that the coding frame can be amended for clarity and robustness. This is often referred to as **double coding**. For the majority of dissertations using **content analysis**, piloting would be recommended, and lower grades may be assigned to students who do not do so, but **double coding** would not always be expected. That said, it should be noted that a limitation of the research would be that the **double coding** was not undertaken.

> **Box 9.1: Student example: positivist framing of content analysis (O'Hare, 2014)**
>
> Going back to Chapter 2, you will recall the importance of **ontology** and research design in documentary analysis. Within Roisin O'Hare's doctoral research on pharmacy education, **content analysis** where 'codes and themes will be derived directly from the reviewed documents' (p 53) was adopted. The researcher noted that: 'The advantage of this approach is the ability to develop themes from the raw data without the potential for preconceived ideas from the literature to prejudice the emergence of new concepts' (p 53). This is a stance that **interpretivist** researchers would

challenge (Braun and Clarke, 2013), but within **positivist ontologies** it would be accepted. Furthermore, the student noted that a proportion of their data was independently coded by a second researcher to increase 'trustworthiness'. Again, this is common in positivistic **content analysis**, but is not seen as beneficial within **content analysis** framed within alternative **ontologies**.

What is thematic analysis and how do I develop themes?

Thematic analysis is a widely used analysis strategy in the social sciences and beyond. Essentially, data are coded, and the researcher then links their knowledge to the codes and broader data set to create themes; results chapters are commonly reported by 'theme', which can be helpful for novice researchers. **Thematic analysis** has been used in a broad variety of ways, ranging from the more positivistic type of **content analysis** reported above to an **interpretivist** analysis that is akin to **discourse analysis**. Because of this considerable variation in use of the term, it can be quite confusing to novice researchers. Victoria Braun and Virginia Clarke (2020), the leading authorities on **thematic analysis**, have proposed a defined approach, which they call **Reflexive Thematic Analysis**. At first glance, **thematic analysis** can appear similar to **content analysis**. However, in Box 9.2, drawing on the work of Braun and Clarke (2020), I highlight the differences between more positivistic attempts at qualitative analysis and interpretivistic **Reflexive Thematic Analysis**.

If you would like an analysis approach with some 'scaffolding' (Braun and Clarke, 2020: 4), within a more critical consideration of the data, a worked example of how to use the technique can be found in Terry et al (2017), drawing on a study of women's experiences of not being a parent.

> ### Box 9.2: Differences between content analysis and Reflexive Thematic Analysis (based on Braun and Clarke, 2020)
>
> While many of the steps in Table 9.1 are aimed at making sure the coding framework is 'correct' and the analysis replicable by another researcher, this is not a component of **thematic analysis** generally, or **Reflexive Thematic Analysis** specifically. This central difference is due to the research paradigm associated with the research. **Content analysis**, when undertaken through a positivistic lens, assumes there *is* a universal truth. Piloting is used to finalise the coding framework *before* the analysis is undertaken. This means that reflections (**inductive** codes) and things that have been missed initially are then excluded from the analysis.

> **Reflexive Thematic Analysis**, however, acknowledges the humanity of researchers, including our variety of backgrounds and experiences (our **positionality**), which we necessarily bring to our analysis. Accordingly, there is no one universal truth (i.e. it is not **positivist** but **interpretivist** in nature) to find. Allowing the introduction of codes throughout the analysis process is known as **inductive** coding and being **reflexive** about this process is strongly encouraged (see Chapter 6). It is definitely my preference to use this approach, always logging at which point in the analysis I have added a new code, so I can go back through the previously coded data to ensure that all data have been considered in relation to all of the codes.

What is discourse analysis and how do I consider meaning in words and images?

Like **content analysis**, there is not one single agreed definition of **discourse analysis**. **Discourse analysis** emphasises studying the language, images and design elements used in depth, with relatively few data extracts compared to a positivistic **content analysis**. We can say that **discourse analysis** therefore searches for deeper **meanings**, or seeks to 'read between the lines', rather than thinking about the content in isolation. Accordingly, within **discourse analysis**, consideration of **meaning** is not restricted to the final phase (as with **content analysis**) but is embedded throughout the entire process. If you are thinking about using an approach such as **discourse analysis**, one thing to consider is whether you should include only text, or any graphical content and images alongside it. Failing to consider the images alongside the words will necessarily change the analysis, as images can be used to imply 'unspeakable' things that would not be written in the text (see Stuart Hall (1997) for further details, and a lovely example by Ball (2010)).

Often considered alongside **discourse analysis** is conversation analysis, which centres interactions. Both approaches arise from ethnomethodology, and strongly focus on uncovering **meaning** through context. While **conversation analysis** focuses on everyday conversational practices, **discourse analysis** focuses on wider society than human-to-human interaction and considers the **semiotics** within speech. Box 9.3 provides an example where images were used alongside words to gain greater understanding of **meaning** using **semiotic analysis**.

How can I use theory to consider the role of documents in shaping behaviour?

There are several different ways that this question could be answered, but my favourite approach is **Actor Network Theory** (Latour, 2005). The purpose of such analysis is to consider the *function* of documents in society. In relation to a

Box 9.3: Considering images in social media analysis of #GivingToIndia

Dickinson (2020) undertook a **semiotic analysis**, that is, looking for signs and signifiers to highlight a **meaning** that is not explicitly stated, relating to foreign and domestic diplomacy in relation to communication via social media. She argues that this public show of diplomacy is a relatively recent way in which to attempt to build diplomatic relations. To give depth to her analysis, she chose one diplomatic relations office serving India. Dickinson's analysis approach focused on visual narratives in the documents, collecting images alongside text by taking manual screenshots of tweets, retweets and Facebook posts. By combining images and text, Dickinson was able to draw conclusions regarding the power relations that influenced the content.

Sketch note 9.2: Creating documents ... influences feelings and behaviour

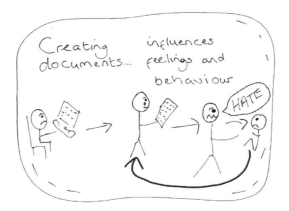

data set under analysis, we would question who are the **authors** and intended **readers** (the 'actors'), and how they interact (how do they form a network?). This **theory** has been adapted from its sociological roots to be applied in very practical ways in social research. In general, **Actor Network Theory** is adopted when researchers have access to both the documents and the individuals who are either the **authors** and/or the intended audience, in order to undertake interviews about how the documents are created and used, or in the form of ethnographic observations. This is an approach that I have taken, as part of a large team within hospitals, to try to reduce the number of children who die in hospital, as described in Box 9.4. This sort of research is likely to be too time-consuming for the average undergraduate dissertation, but it is one of the most valuable ways to understand **meaning** within documents.

> **Box 9.4: Using Actor Network Theory in paediatric wards, to understand clinical decisions**
>
> Within the PUMA study, myself and some other researchers spent time on UK paediatric wards observing the behaviour of staff, including doctors and nurses. This included seeing what, when and how they documented how well the children in their care were. Matching up the second part of **Actor Network Theory**, we considered how staff who were new to looking after that patient reviewed the notes and how they treated the patient. Analysis of the collected data allowed a new quality improvement intervention to be designed, with communication between staff as a component (see Allen et al, in press).

What if I want to use a type of analysis that isn't covered here?

There are many types of analysis, and different names for similar types of analysis between academic disciplines. This often occurs because they draw on **theory** from that discipline. It would be impossible to cover all the analysis strategies here. However, that is not to say that other analysis approaches are not high quality or useful. My advice if you wish to follow an alternative strategy is to follow a methodological guide to ensure you undertake high-quality analysis. An example of an analysis approach that I was not previously familiar with can be found in Box 9.5 in relation to the marketing of opera in the UK.

> **Box 9.5: Using a paratextual analysis to identify and contextualise advertising**
>
> An example of research that considered the contents of contemporary documents against historical references is Grainger and Minier's (2019) research on marketing from opera companies toward potential audiences. They chose a **sample** of contemporary marketing materials directed toward audiences from one theatre company's production of three plays referred to as the 'Tudors Trilogy'. Their analysis focused on the use of 'heritagising' (p 30) within the advertising, using markers to suggest that the operas were relatable to the Tudor period, and not restricted to traditional opera audiences. They argue that the aim of this was to create a brand that was chic and accessible in a retro way.

How do I decide if I need to use theory?

In Chapter 2 we discussed integrating **theory** with **epistemology**, **ontology** and research paradigms; you may wish to revisit Chapter 2 for a more thorough account. Documentary analysis is such a flexible tool for research that it can be used both with and without **theory**. Likewise, **content analysis** and **thematic analysis** can be used with and without **theory**. Within social policy and public health, the disciplines where I mostly work, **theory** is often not used. In other disciplines, such as sociology, criminology and education, it is more common, and a lack of **theory** may be considered a sign of a lack of analytical skill on your part. Because of this, I strongly recommend that you return to Chapter 2, and consider potential theories from your discipline and proactively make notes of the theoretical lens (if any) that has been used in the literature in your literature review. Before making any big decisions, discuss your ideas with your supervisor if possible. Within Box 9.6, an analysis of the use of Disabled people in advertising is contextualised within feminist disability studies, which included a Disabled researcher co-analysing the data with Disabled people through interviews.

> ### Box 9.6: The influence of theory on analysis: disability in advertising
>
> An example of a researcher using documentary analysis choosing to use **theory** is in a study of media portrayals of Disabled women in advertising, by Ella Houston (2019). If including **theory** is an area that concerns you in relation to your dissertation, you may wish to read the methods section of her paper to understand how she applied **theory** to her documentary analysis. Houston notes early in her methods section that feminist disability studies has been used. For those unfamiliar, she gives a few lines of detail, including rejecting positivism and aiming to empower Disabled women. To do so, she notes that, in addition to her own analysis, semi-structured interviews were undertaken with Disabled women in which they undertook a document-facilitated interview, where their opinions were elicited through viewing advertisements. As part of her commitment to feminist disability studies, she notes that, in her results section, direct quotations and long narrative accounts are provided from the five Disabled women interviewed, so that her influence on the analysis was less dominant.

Why would I want to triangulate my analysis?

Triangulation is another term without a set **meaning**. It can mean using more than one set of the same type of document, such as two newspapers' coverage of the same item. It can also mean using more than one type of document to find out about a thing. For example, looking into historical **archives**, you may find documents written by the parish council, maps and personal correspondence that you may use together to consider an issue from multiple perspectives. Finally, **triangulation** could mean using documentary analysis *alongside* another research method, such as interviews or observations. You can use your existing documentary analysis skills to undertake the first two types of **triangulation** by simply comparing and contrasting the different sources. However, the third type, involving the use of at least one extra social research method, is likely to be beyond the scope of most undergraduate dissertations, or will need a small **sample** size to fit within the time available.

Speaking with creators or users of documents is usually formalised into a structured, semi-structured or unstructured interview (as in Houston, 2019; see Box 9.6). I recommend a semi-structured approach if your plan is to find out about the documents' creation and use. Interviewing is a specialist skill, and if you have not interviewed a participant for a research study before, you should review relevant literature (e.g. Mason, 2018) and practical guidance (e.g. Kara, 2018b), and consider practising with a friend first. You should also carefully consider the contents of your interview topic guide to ensure that it is aligned with your **research questions**. In terms of practicalities, ensure that you always have a reliable way of recording your interview, and preferably a back-up as well. You will almost certainly need to obtain ethical approval and informed consent if you include interviews within your research project.

Observing those who are creating or using the documents, sometimes referred to as nonparticipant observation, is even more specialist than interviewing them. This is because you will often have very limited control over what happens, which can be overwhelming for the novice researcher. You will also need to find a way to record what you observe, either by taking notes, or committing things to memory, and writing them down at a later date. These notes are known as 'fieldnotes'. One of the hardest things that researchers (of all levels) experience is being tired from having been 'in the field' but still having the discipline to make and expand on notes while events are still fresh in your mind. An overview of the core concepts and how to undertake observations can be found in Atkinson's chapter 'Fieldwork commitments' (Atkinson, 2015: 33–45).

Why doesn't software '*do*' my analysis for me?

You may have heard a dangerous myth that there is software that will *do* your qualitative analysis for you. The software does not *do* any of the analysis, and it definitely cannot be your analysis strategy, as some quantitative researchers believe. Instead, you could imagine a qualitative data analysis software program as a big scrapbook, where *you* virtually cut and paste data extracts; the computer cannot do that for you. The benefit of qualitative data analysis software (known

Sketch note 9.3: The joy of hand coding

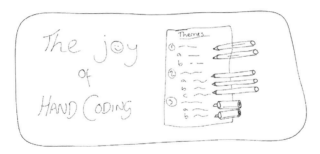

as **CAQDAS**) is that it helps you to bring together all the data relating to the particular labels you have given them. However, there can still be elements of human error, and also the dreaded corruption of your analysis files (akin to leaving hard copies on the train). For this reason, if you are using **CAQDAS**, make regular back-ups.

If you have not used one of these specialist computer programs – such as **NVivo** or **ATLAS.ti** – before analysing your dissertation data, it is sensible to weigh up the pros and cons of learning how to use a new computer program. You could consider whether it: will save you any time or, make you feel any more confident that you haven't missed an important piece of data, or if it is simply accepted as good practice in your department such that **hand coding** would appear unusual to your examiner. That isn't to say that using software is more reliable or valid than hand coding, and I code by hand on smaller projects, where I find it is more manageable.

Conclusion

This chapter has contained a very brief overview of an enormous amount of information. Multiple books have been written about each of the analysis strategies discussed here, so if you feel overwhelmed or confused, this is totally normal. Hopefully, having read the background and theoretical information in part one of the chapter, and engaged with the practical exploration of **content**, **discourse** and **thematic analysis**, you have an idea of one or two analysis strategies that you would definitely like to rule out. We have also briefly considered the role of **theory** in your analysis, and you should have an idea of whether you will use a particular **theory** prior to setting your **research question** and collecting your data. Another practical step for you to consider is the use of computer software or hard copies of your data to facilitate your analysis; remember the computer doesn't *do* the analysis for you. The next chapter pulls together the knowledge from the three previous chapters in Part II to write your **research questions** and your methods chapter.

Further reading

Undergraduate

Chin, B.A. (2004) *How to Write a Great Research Paper*, Hoboken, NJ: John Wiley & Son.

Largan, C. and Morris, T. (2019) *Qualitative Secondary Research*, London: SAGE. Chapter 11: Analysing data pp 231–255.

Postgraduate

Braun, V. and Clarke, V. (2019) 'Reflecting on reflexive thematic analysis', *Qualitative Research in Sport, Exercise and Health*, 11(4): 589–597.

Grant, A. (2019) *Doing Excellent Social Research with Documents: Practical Examples and Guidance for Qualitative Researchers*, Abingdon: Routledge.

10

Writing research questions and your methods chapter

Summary

Your dissertation is centred around the one little sentence that is your **research question**, so it's important to get it right. This chapter starts by providing strategies to understand what a 'research gap' is (hint: it's pretty broad as long as you are not situated within a **positivist** research paradigm). It will then move on to examine the core components of a **research question**, before considering how to draft your own. Finally, we will consider what should be included in your methods chapter.

Objectives

By reading this chapter, you should understand:

- what a 'research gap' is;
- what the core components of a **research question** are;
- how to write a **research question**;
- what to include in your methods chapter.

Introduction: Why your research question is the most important sentence in your dissertation

Research questions are important.

I'm going to say that again: **research questions** are really, really important. You can think of your **research question** as the ball in any ball-game: without it you have lots of skilled people and a pitch, but no way to play or win the game. Let's think about this in relation to the chapters of your dissertation (Box 10.1). As always, please do write notes in your research diary as you read through this chapter – those little flashes of inspiration are really important, especially when writing your **research question**, which needs to be small but mighty.

Sketch note 10.1: Research questions are central to your dissertation

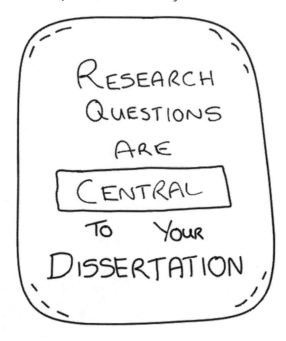

RESEARCH
QUESTIONS
ARE
CENTRAL
TO YOUR
DISSERTATION

Box 10.1: Does your research question fit with the content in your dissertation chapters?

Consider your draft research question in relation to its fit with each of your chapters:

1. Introduction: why your **research question** is important.
2. Literature review: should point to your **research question** as almost like an arrow highlighting a group of interesting phenomena being brought together (or a funnel: see Chapter 7 for a refresher) to which the only logical conclusion *is* your **research question**.
3. Methods: your **population, sample** (including size) and analysis methods are clearly designed to enable the **research question** to be answered. The **research question** should fit the methods exactly.
4. Results: describe your findings in a way that explicitly shows your new contribution to knowledge in relation to the **research question**.
5. Discussion: compares the literature in your literature review chapter, which led you to the **research question** in the first place, and provides a space to identify similarities and differences between your findings and the literature.
6. Conclusion: disentangles the importance of the topic area, the methods, **research question** and new findings to say, with confidence, that your **research question** and research were important.

The process of going from lots of information to a **research question** can be very hard and you may feel that you hate your dissertation. That is completely normal. If you have time, try to make some rough notes about your **research question**'s contents and then take a break. If you only have a short time, go outside, spend time cooking, do some exercise; whatever will take your mind out of the dissertation for a while, and then come back to it. It should feel a bit easier. If not it's time to book a supervision or catch up with a peer. Your dissertation will feel easier once you're past this decision-making 'hump'.

What is the scope of a dissertation project?

The scope, or boundaries, of a dissertation can be considered in two ways: first, the intellectual scope of what is expected. This is for a **research question** to be rationalised (by the beginning of your dissertation) and then answered effectively (the methods chapter onwards of your dissertation). In Box 10.1, some hints are given for ensuring that each chapter of your dissertation fits within the scope. Alongside the practical boundaries of answering your **research question**, making a novel contribution to knowledge is often required. This is in terms of the analytical leaps you make between bodies of literature and how you answer your **research question**.

Second, the scope of a dissertation in terms of size and complexity varies considerably between level (undergraduate, master's, doctorate) and institution. Undergraduate dissertations are sometimes 5,000 words or fewer but can be 12,000 words or more. The word limit will impact on the boundaries you set yourself, to allow adequate 'weight' in terms of words and time to each of your chapters. Techniques to facilitate this are discussed in Chapter 3, and I recommend returning to that chapter or your own planning documents to make your dissertation balanced.

What is a 'research gap'?

A research gap is where there is no published research on a particular topic or subtopic. The concept of a research gap is aligned within positivistic **epistemologies**; within more **interpretivist** or pragmatist approaches, a research gap occurs simply because society is ever-evolving, so there is always something new to be discovered. Research gaps do not need to be overstated if the gap is small, or made very narrow if the gap is large. For example, in Nino Amonashvili's (2011: 4) master's dissertation on education policy in Georgia, he notes: 'There is a lack of scientific research on education in Georgia. It is hard to find a valid analysis of the whole process of development and implementation of a reform and there is almost no further evaluation done.'

An alternative way to considering whether you have a 'gap' comes from Peter Levin (2005: 38), who argues that your **research question** and plan should be something that:

- you're enthusiastic about;
- you're likely to be able to do;
- will likely produce interesting conclusions;
- is specific enough so the question can be answered;
- is narrow enough that the question can be answered in the time you have available;
- can be expressed as a clear research aim.

This process can be viewed through the work of Sissel Waagen's (2016) dissertation on passports in Norway (Box 10.2).

Box 10.2: Student example: why study Norwegian passports? (Waagen, 2016)

Sissel Waagen's master's dissertation provides a clear rationale for the topic under study in the introduction:

- Passports are understudied in the social sciences (p 8).
- Within the context of the 9/11 terrorist attacks in America, the study of *risk* became heightened, particularly in relation to border control (p 9).
- Passport privilege and freedom of movement are privileges that some people have, and others do not. Waagen recognises her privilege which she relates to a Norwegian passport, and compares it to a lack of privilege for colleagues from other countries (p 7).
- Passports have changed considerably over time, and link to mass electronic data sets now, while previously they were handwritten paper artefacts (p 8).

She moves on to provide four **research questions** (p 10) that link to this topic and the rationale behind studying this topic.

If you are in a department where dissertations are required to follow a format where a research gap is discovered before the research is designed, the good news is that within documentary analysis, there is nearly always a range of research gaps available. This includes areas where lots of research has already been done. Research gaps include:

- a sub-topic that has not been explored in the literature;
- a new way of analysing documents that have already been analysed;

- a change in society's views, or a new law, policy or programme;
- your unique perspective as a lay or professional person with knowledge of the topic.

Traditional 'literature gaps'

When you read the literature review of a dissertation or journal article, you may notice a flow between topics that brings you to a very logical **research question**. However, this is not a happy accident; the **reader** just doesn't get to see the effort required to get to the end point. In the case of finding a research gap, this takes a lot of critical thinking from the researcher if they are looking for a gap in the literature. With so many journals and so much research being undertaken, there are fewer large gaps to be explored than even 20 years ago. What you often find are sub-topics, where something within a category has been studied, but not every element of that category. For example, if you find that there has been lots of literature on the marketing of pet food for dogs and cats, a little bit on birds but none on rodents, you could use that gap to justify looking at marketing of food for hamsters, or rats, or guinea pigs (or capybaras, the largest and most magnificent rodent of them all). Alternatively, if this topic has been investigated in one country but not another, that could be of interest.

Sketch note 10.2: Find the (research) gap

New ways of analysing old topics or documents

As well as an unexplored research area, you can bring a new form of analysis to an area that has already been investigated. Three commonly used forms of analysis were outlined in Chapter 9. Returning to our idea of marketing of pet food, if a very large piece of **content analysis** had been conducted on adverts for cat food in Brazil, a new study might use **discourse analysis** on a smaller **sample**, reviewing the words to 'read between the lines' and considering how the images and graphics were designed to be 'read' by the intended audience, including, for example, the breed of cat, fullness of its coat, the location and the food bowl used (if any).

Changes in society

No matter what has come before your dissertation, there is nearly always a way to find a gap in a crowded research area. For example, if a policy changes, a topic may become contentious, and this increased relevance can create the importance necessary to justify your research. Considering our pet food marketing project, some potentially interesting changes include:

- a new law mandating certain vitamins are included in cat food;
- increased ownership of dogs during the COVID-19 lockdown and whether the adverts are different from previously; or
- a celebrity (such as the new US President at the time of writing, Joe Biden) having a rescue dog, rather than a pedigree from a breeder.

New perspectives

Another way that you may be able to find a novel angle in a crowded area of research is if you bring your own lay or professional knowledge of the topic to bear. This technique is most often used within autoethnographic research (literally an **ethnography** in which part of your life is the data) and research by practitioners, such as those in health and education fields. For example, teachers undertaking a master's degree in education will often undertake a dissertation in which they change an element of practice within their own classrooms. This could include using different textbooks and seeing what happens, undertaking a **discourse analysis** of the contents of the old and new textbooks. A second way in which new perspectives can be brought is when marginalised groups bring their own experiences to the research field. For example, Jenny Thatcher's (2020) **ethnography** of a working-class 'wet lead' (i.e. not typically a place for a meal) public house (more typically known as a 'pub') in London. Thatcher's background as a working-class academic with ongoing experience of working in a pub is valuable in her documentary analysis of policy documents and speeches, where she can bring lived experience to the middle-class professional politicians' discourses.

Sketch note 10.3: Look for cultural change

How do I write a research question?

One structure to consider when creating a **research question** is to ask What? Who? When? Where? and Why? (see Box 10.3) To bring the framework in Box 10.3 to life, I have created Resource 10.1 (also available online).

Example 1: Racism in the media; initial thoughts on a research question

In order to examine how I used Resource 10.1, let's think about a study of 'The portrayal of race in the media', aiming to establish the presence of various forms of racism (this has long been studied, with little improvement: see Hall's 1997 analysis of this very thing). Table 10.1 includes the questions from Box 10.3 in the first column, asks some additional conceptual and high-level questions in the second column, with some potential responses to the questions – some

> **Box 10.3: Writing a research question using what, who, when, where and why**
>
> - *What* topic area?
> - *Who* are the documents written by?
> - *When* are the documents from?
> - *Where* are the documents from?
> - *Why* is this research important?

Resource 10.1: Writing your research question

Research question element	Questions and influences	Types of documents to consider
What topic area?		
Who are the documents, or the type / **authors** of the documents?		
When are the documents from (which time period)?		
Where are the documents from?		
Why is this research important?		

of which are simply more questions – in the third column. You may find that Resource 10.1 facilitates your consideration of the elements of your **research question**.

Example 2: Planning applications for student housing; unpicking the research question

As this is difficult to get right, and we know that it is important for the quality of your dissertation, I'm going to give you a second example where I describe my process of drafting a **research question**, and then show you the question's contents which relate to each of the five questions in Box 10.3.

Table 10.1: Considerations when designing a research question on racism and the media

Research question element	Questions and influences regarding studying racism in the media	Types of document to consider and other thoughts
What topic area?	What do we mean by racism? What do we mean by media?	Need to review existing literature to see where there are potential research gaps.
Who are the documents created by?	Documents produced *by* the media	Newspapers, magazines, social media content, etc. Are we considering media from **journalists**, **bloggers** or the public via social media?
	Documents produced *about* the media relating to race/discrimination	Court documents, government inquiries, third sector reviews of practice.
When are the documents from?	Contemporary or historical?	This will really influence the **research question** and the data collected. Need to develop a solid rationale for the period of time.
Where are the documents from?	Local news or national news? My country or another country?	Do I have enough knowledge to understand the context? Do I need local (or even hyperlocal, such as **blogs**) or national sources to answer my question?
	Two or more countries with comparison?	Is there value in comparing multiple countries? If yes, do I have time to do this in sufficient detail or will the analysis be too superficial?
Why is this research important?	Who is the intended readership? What size is the intended readership? What influence could these documents have on the intended and unintended readership?	Why is this particular story or type of racism within this specific type of media more important than other possible investigations? NB: include some of this contextual information in your introduction chapter.

Imagine I was investigating the decisions of planning offices within local councils in relation to student accommodation. Over the past decade, this has been an issue in Cardiff, where I live. Large high-rise halls of residence are built, with tiny rooms, no parking and little access to amenities (usually residential accommodation in the UK would require parking and access to amenities as a legal requirement). Some of these buildings are already requesting 'change of use' due to lack of demand, so that anybody could live there.

I could shrink my topic to fit my available time by only considering one or two councils or specifying a time period. Another way to be specific is to consider the size of developments that would be included: would small developments of (say) fewer than ten rooms be relevant, or are only very large high-rise buildings of interest? I need to consider what I am trying to find out: why is this research topic important? I would say that it is about how councils can justify these developments, knowing that there is an excess of accommodation already. The keyword in that sentence is *justify*; that means I'm interested in written texts and the language used. Documents of interest would, therefore, be everything produced by the developer and the council, focused on a relatively smaller number of documents so that I can undertake **discourse analysis**. As this appears to be a relatively recent phenomenon, I might compare and contrast recent cases with older cases. Bearing all of this in mind, my **research question** could be:

> How do developers and local councillors justify building new high rise student accommodation, and has this changed over time? A **discourse analysis** of planning applications and decisions in Cardiff from 2000 to 2020.

Going back to the bullet points in Box 10.3, in Table 10.2 we can see what each element of the **research question** does. Within the table, I have copied and pasted the full **research question** and highlighted the relevant sections, using bold and underlining, an approach you may find useful.

Before you finalise the data to use within your project and your analysis approach, it is important to have a clear idea of what your *specific* research focus is. I recommend writing a draft of your **research question** and checking it with your supervisor. A bad **research question** can make good research look mediocre, particularly within positivistic paradigms, as it does not answer the question it was supposed to.

What should I include in my methods chapter?

This varies from discipline to discipline. Within the module handbook for your dissertation, you may find an example structure for your methods chapter.

Table 10.2: Developing a research question on planning applications for student halls of residence

Research question element	Planning applications study
What topic area?	How do developers and local councillors justify building new **high rise student accommodation**, and has this changed over time? A **discourse analysis** of **planning applications and decisions** in Cardiff from 2000 to 2020.
Who are the documents created by?	How do **developers and local councillors** justify building new high rise student accommodation, and has this changed over time? A **discourse analysis** of **planning applications and decisions** in Cardiff from 2000 to 2020.
When are the documents from?	How do developers and local councillors justify building new high rise student accommodation, and has this changed over time? A **discourse analysis** of planning applications and decisions in Cardiff from **2000 to 2020.**
Where are the documents from?	How do developers and local councillors justify building new high rise student accommodation, and has this changed over time? A **discourse analysis** of planning applications and decisions in **Cardiff** from 2000 to 2020.
Why is this research important?	How do developers and local councillors **justify** building new high rise student accommodation, and has this changed over time? A **discourse analysis** of planning applications and decisions in Cardiff from 2000 to 2020.

Sketch note 10.4: Celebrate identifying your research question

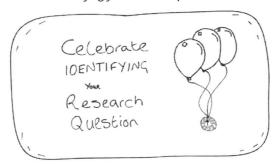

High-quality dissertations are often placed in university libraries and online **archives**, so you could find a dissertation using a qualitative analysis approach and examine its structure. A third option is to examine the methods section of journal articles from your discipline: how much space do they give to their methods section, *relative to the length of the paper*? I direct you to these sources because you *are not* writing an essay for a research methods class, but a scientific report of the research you undertook, in order to allow it to be fully understood by your examiner – and in some disciplines leaning more toward a quantitative, positivistic **epistemology**, to replicate your research. Box 10.4 provides one structure that I personally would use in a methods chapter (please note that this is not the only way or the 'correct way').

Box 10.4: How I would structure a methods chapter

- If you have not stated your **research question** at the end of the literature review, do so at the beginning of your chapter.
- If you have an **epistemology**, **ontology** or theoretical framework that you have not yet declared, do so near the beginning of the chapter.
- **Population** and sampling decisions. In some disciplines, this is followed by a description of your **sample**; in others, this is the first section of your results chapter.
- Data collection and any preparation required prior to analysis.
- Analysis strategy, including reference to the particular type you are using, and an overview of the steps included.
- Any piloting.
- Ethical considerations.

As with your literature review chapter, it is best to 'throw some words on the page' at this stage, so that you have *something* for each section. In Chapter 3, we considered how to split your dissertation word count by chapter. It is also sensible to consider word limits *within* chapters. For example, if you have 2,000–2,500 words for your methods chapter, you may wish to divide those 2,000–2,500 words across your sub-headings in a way that is similar to the dissertations that do well within your department. If it were my dissertation, I would split my word count as shown in Box 10.5. My total is 1,750 words, because I know that I am always a bit over the word count in each section, giving me margin for error in a section intended to be 2,000 words long.

Box 10.5: Word count for sub-sections within Aimee's (pretend) dissertation

- Introduction – one paragraph, 150 words
- **Research question** – 50 words
- Theoretical perspective – one paragraph, 250 words
- **Population** and **sample** – one paragraph, 250 words
- Data collection and data management – one paragraph, 250 words
- Analysis strategy – one paragraph, 250 words
- Implementation of analysis strategy – one paragraph, 250 words
- Any piloting – n/a
- Ethical considerations – one paragraph, 250 words
- Signposting to next section – 50 words
- Contingency – 250 words

Resource 10.2: Structuring your methods chapter

Section	Paragraph details/ purpose	Planned word count	Details
Introduction (1 paragraph)			
Research question			NB: only if not included at the end of your literature review chapter
Epistemology, ontology and theory			If applicable
Population and sampling			
Data collection			
Data analysis			
Piloting			If applicable
Ethical considerations			
Conclusion (1 paragraph)			

Conclusion

Part II of this book has contained *a lot* of information and will need processing if the information is new to you. In this final chapter of Part II, we have considered how to put together all the information relating to literature, sources and analysis strategy, into a **research question**. This **research question** is the foundation for your dissertation so, if at all possible, don't rush it. We have examined different types of research gaps, and what information should be in a **research question**. Through two examples, I have considered how you could put this information into practice. Finally, we looked at what to include within the methods chapter of your dissertation, and a way of deciding on the sub-headings you will use and their relative word counts. In Part III, we move on to considering collecting, managing and analysing data, as well as writing your two other major chapters, Findings and Discussion.

Further reading

Undergraduate

O'Leary, Z. (2018) *Little Quick Fix: Research Questions*, London: SAGE.
White, P. (2009) *Developing Research Questions: A Guide for Social Scientists*, Basingstoke: Palgrave Macmillan, pp 33–58.
Yin, R.K. (2011) *Qualitative Research from Start to Finish*, London: The Guildford Press, pp 49–74.

Postgraduate

Alvesson, M. and Sandberg, J. (2013) *Constructing Research Questions: Doing Interesting Research*, London: SAGE.
White, P. (2009) *Developing Research Questions: A Guide for Social Scientists*, Basingstoke: Palgrave Macmillan.

PART III

Getting it done!

Part III is about actually *doing* the research, building on your literature searching, reading and writing from Part II, and assumes that you have already:

- identified your research paradigm;
- reviewed relevant literature and begun drafting your full literature review chapter;
- considered if you should use a theoretical perspective in your research, and decided on the **theory** if relevant;
- planned a data analysis strategy, which informed how much data to include in your **sample**;
- found data that can answer your **research question**; and
- drafted your methods chapter.

Along the way, you have (hopefully!) written notes in a research diary of some sort, undertaken tasks and used some of the resources provided – amending them to the requirements for your department. These should give you the information you need to write your literature review and methods chapters.

In Part III, we add to this solid foundation by:

- understanding how best to organise information about the data you have collected and your analysis, in order to draft your results chapter;
- considering issues of quality and **bias** within your **sample**, and what to include in your discussion chapter; and finally
- looking at how to pull together everything you have created into a final dissertation report, including incorporating feedback from your supervisors.

As always, you need to keep in mind the content from Part I. This stage, when deadlines are looming, can be a point when students feel very stressed and can often benefit from support from supervisors (Chapter 4), peers or other forms of self-care (Chapter 6).

Likewise, if you have been delayed and are not in line with the plan you developed in Chapter 2, you may want to revisit it and divide up your remaining time so that you can still draw robust conclusions from your analysis. These will be shown in your discussion chapter and are important for securing higher grades. One of the core paths to success is to make sure you keep writing.

Below I give a short overview of the contents of each chapter. Remember, as always, you do not have to read the book in full and can read the chapters in whichever order feels most valuable.

Sketch note PIII.1: Do some writing today

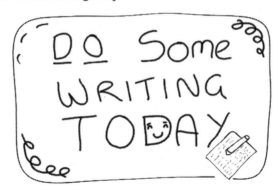

Detailed description of chapters

Chapter 11

Chapter 11 focuses on data collection and ensuring good practice in terms of data security. This is known as data management. Data management is nearly always overlooked, as it is not particularly 'researchy' (you're right, that isn't actually a word, but I'm going to use it anyway) as a skill. However, not backing up your data and analysis can cost you a lot of time and effort if you get it wrong. Moving on to the dissertation itself, I outline ways of showing the core elements of your **sample**, similar to demographic details (age, gender, employment status, etc.) that are included in the reporting on research on human subjects. This is an important skill if your examiner does not usually use documents in their research practice, to show your research is **robust**. We then move on to consider how to code data, which is a skill used in the majority of qualitative analysis strategies, before thinking about what to include within your results chapter.

Chapter 12

Jennifer Platt (1981a, 1981b) famously noted that using documents as data resulted in different **biases** than other qualitative methods. In Chapter 12, we focus on quality and sources of **bias** within the documents in your **sample**. You may feel panicky that your data are poor quality, but at the undergraduate and even master's level, with the time constraints involved, it is usual to have a **sample** that has significant **biases**: you just need to report what they are, to show your understanding of good research practice. Following this methodical analysis of your data, which is included in the 'strengths and weaknesses' part of your discussion chapter, we consider what else belongs in your discussion chapter, the last of your major chapters.

Chapter 13

Editing your draft chapters, including responding to supervisors' comments and inserting new information, is a challenge for the most accomplished writer. As such, Chapter 13 focuses on going from your notes and draft chapters to getting your dissertation ready to submit. I describe a range of methods to get yourself in 'the zone' of writing and highlight ways in which you may struggle with feedback from your supervisor. Once the writing is over, it is time for the fiddly bits of formatting, including 'front matter' such as declarations that the work is your own, and appendices, such as copies of some of your data or an extract from your analysis. The final step before submission is a review of your work for clarity and coherence, followed by proofreading.

Chapter 14

In Chapter 14, I say a brief farewell to you, and wish you all the best with your dissertation. I decided that this book would be unbalanced without a conclusion, so I included one. Like the concluding chapters of dissertations and the conclusions you see in journal articles, it is pretty short and doesn't contain any new information!

Collecting and analysing data and writing your results chapter

Summary

This chapter introduces the craft of *doing* research, that is, the little tips and tricks that make you successful at collecting and analysing data, separate to the methodological and empirical knowledge that helps you to write a good methods chapter. This includes things like backing up your work (go on, do a quick back-up now!) and creating a catalogue or database of each of your pieces of data, including key information. Moving on to your results chapter, I show you how to create a table summarising the characteristics of your documents, and an approach to structuring the rest of your chapter.

Objectives

By reading this chapter, you should understand:

- why it is vital to regularly back up your work;
- which information you should be recording about each of your documents;
- how coding is different to an analysis strategy;
- how to code your data;
- what to include in your results chapter.

Introduction: The horror of losing data or text!

Data management is not an exciting topic, but it can save you hours and hours. If you do not back up your work and then have some sort of accident, you may be left without a copy of your most recent work. Can you remember when you last backed up your work? How many hours of work have you put into your dissertation since then?

I wasn't always as good at backing up my work as I am now. In Box 11.1, I describe the day that I thought I would need to quit my PhD because my USB stick was empty when I opened it.

Sketch note 11.1: Back up your work

Box 11.1: The day I thought I'd lost all of my data, and why I don't want you to feel this way!

This is an example of how *not* to manage your data. Please learn from my mistake; when I think of it now, I can still feel that complete dread wash over me!

When I was doing my PhD, I interviewed participants, undertook nonparticipant observation, and analysed patient case files. One day, I came into the office, plugged my trusty USB stick (they were reasonably new and cool at the time and thought to be considerably more reliable than CDs or floppy disks) into my aged university computer. When I opened the file explorer, expecting to see all the interviews that I had conducted so far, there was nothing. I wrote in my research diary,

> I can't possibly collect that data again. Those people will never say the same things even if they will let me speak to them again. All of those hours of scanning patient files: lost. I'll need to drive (250 miles) to get another copy!

My officemate at the time (the outstanding Dawn Mannay: check out her work (e.g. Mannay, 2016) if you are interested in visual methods) wasn't in that day. I turned on her computer, plugged in my USB stick and all my folders were visible. None of my data were lost. I immediately backed up my files onto the university's cloud-based network and was beyond happy to discover that it had been a false alarm.

Sketch note 11.2: Create a filing system – and use it

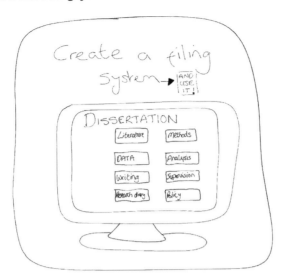

At the beginning of your project, set up a basic filing system within a cloud-based network (I suggest your university's network, which will be the most secure and definitely compliant with data protection laws and your ethical approval) to make sure you never have that feeling of having lost your data (or even worse, *actually* lose it).

How can I keep on track?

In Chapter 2, we made lots of plans. By now these may have been deviated from, due to the difficulty of predicting timescales in research, when there are so many different variables. At this stage, if you have fallen behind where you planned to be, I suggest that you do a quick recalculation. Look at your self-imposed deadlines for each chapter on a **Gantt chart**, calendar or list: are they still looking realistic? Do you have any new major conflicts?

Alongside this, in Chapter 2, I suggested you set up an online folder (preferably in a cloud-based system) and gave you a structure that might be helpful for storing your work. If you haven't already done this, now – before you collect your data – would be an excellent time to do so. I usually have a sub-folder in each of my project folders, which I call DATA. I tend to use capital letters in file names as a way of drawing attention to the importance of them. Sometimes I number folders sequentially, so that the order of research projects is apparent. You can use whatever strategy works for you, as long as you have a strategy.

What information should I be recording when collecting data?

When considering the documents that could be used as data in your project in Chapter 8, we thought about the types of search strategies that you could use in

Sketch note 11.3: Don't panic: plan!

online **archives**, on the internet, and through personal contacts. The information in Chapter 8 was about identifying a **sample**. Now you've identified a **sample**, it's time to:

- document your decisions around *why* these documents were included and why others were excluded;
- save a copy of each document;
- record some details about the data individually and as a whole.

This information can generally be found toward the beginning of your results chapter, although it is sometimes included in your '**sample**' section of the methods chapter. This all occurs *before* you dive into analysis.

Decisions around including or excluding documents

This depends on the research paradigm (e.g. **positivist** vs. **interpretivist**) that your project is using. You should *always* have a solid rationale as to why some documents were included while others that could have been used to answer your **research question** were not. If you are finding it hard to think through your decision, you might find writing about the different documents in your research diary, or even speaking aloud to yourself (you can record yourself so you don't miss any brilliant thoughts) can help you to process the complexities of the sources that you think are best suited to answer your question.

In more positivistic paradigms, such as within healthcare, a particular template is sometimes used to show these decisions. For example, see Hoyle et al's (2018) work on media reporting of violence against nurses. The flow chart used by

Sketch note 11.4: Don't forget to write things down

Hoyle et al. (2018) and displayed in Figure 11.1 originates from the PRISMA flow chart (Moher et al, 2009), originally designed for people undertaking systematic reviews, a very positivistic form of literature reviewing. The flow chart takes the **reader** through four stages: identifying documents, screening (an initial examination to see if the document is suitable), eligibility (a more detailed examination of documents that may be relevant) and finally the documents included in the **sample**. Even if using the diagram itself isn't useful to you, it does provide a clear way of establishing how you got from the **population** to your **sample**. Figure 11.1 is an example of a PRISMA flow chart from a research project I mentioned in Chapter 8 (see Box 8.5) considering how the media database **Nexis®** was used to identify documents in international English-language newspapers examining views of breast milk sharing among peers.

The two reasons why articles were excluded (seen in the boxes on the right-hand side of Figure 11.1) were that they were duplicated content or 'irrelevant'. In the text alongside the diagram, we explained within the body of the article that content was irrelevant if it did not meet all three of these criteria:

> Focused primarily on peer-to-peer breastmilk sharing *and*
> Focused on breastmilk sharing for the benefit of infants *and*
> English Language. (Dowling and Grant, 2021: 4)

The need for a 'clean' set of data

This is important: you always, always want to save a set of your data, and not touch it again.
You then copy the 'data' folder contents into your analysis folder. This means that if you happen to delete a document (or alter it by mistake), you have an original copy to which you can easily return. It also means that if anything 'funny'

seems to happen (e.g. your document doesn't seem to match its demographic information – see below), you can check which information is incorrect. Some **CAQDAS** programs will automatically make a new copy of the data for you, but others do not, so I recommend that you create a second copy to ensure that no data can be lost if your analysis file corrupts.

Naming conventions for your data

I am a fan of **Document Identification Numbers (DINs)** with any data I collect; in Box 11.2 I provide an example of my use of DINs and brief descriptors in a study of magazine awards given to mother and baby products. I tend to start at one and increase the number sequentially. If I am using data from more than

Figure 11.1: An example of a PRISMA flow chart, based on Dowling and Grant, 2021

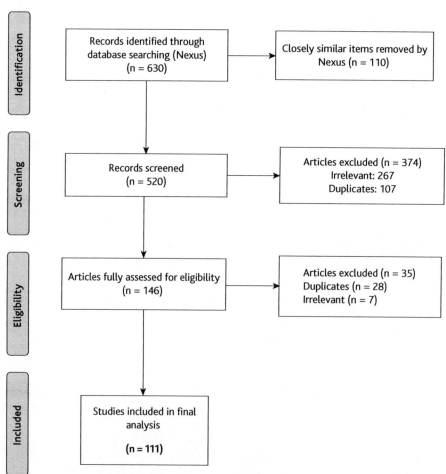

Sketch note 11.5: Be methodical and organised

one **author**, or multiple types, I may use an initial to note which **author**. Often, especially if I am working alone and not having to share the data, I will give it a brief description, such as 'letter red umbrella' for a letter that contained lots of details, one of which was the red umbrella that stuck in my mind, and this helps me to imagine the **author**, **reader** and their relationship. Finally, I date all of my documents if there is any likelihood of them changing over time, such as with newspaper articles and web pages.

Within my 'DATA' folder, I have downloaded many of the documents as both PDF (to show the original layout of images and text on the web pages) and Word documents, which I find makes them more manageable for textual analysis within **ATLAS.ti**, the **CAQDAS** program I intend to use for this research project. For PB3, you can see that I have left myself a methodological note in the filename ('image only no text included on page'). Use any convention that works for you.

When I have all my data ready for analysis, I will copy and paste the entire DATA folder into my analysis folder, and do not use these 'clean' documents again unless there is a problem.

Describing your sample

It is important to be able to describe some basic information about your **sample**. This isn't part of your analysis but akin to the 'demographics' section in research with people. Depending on your discipline, this may be noted in the text, or presented in a table, either with the characteristics of each document, or the overall characteristics of your **sample**. Items may relate to a range of characteristics seen in Box 11.3. Combining your **sample**'s characteristics and discussing the **sample** as a whole is often done to protect anonymity when there are small **samples** involving individuals. The information to include within your description will vary

Box 11.2: Naming conventions for documents in a study of mother and baby product awards

Within this research project, I used three magazines. I named them by their first initials: B, M_B (because an '&' sign cannot be used in a filename) and PB. Most of the content related to the 2020 awards, although some related to 2019 or 2021. I used the following format:

1. initial to represent magazine;
2. sequential number by magazine (e.g. there is a B1 and also an M_B1 and PB1);
3. which year's award ceremony the content related to;
4. a short descriptor to help me remember the contents.

Example names include:

- B1 – 2019 awards – all about our awards
- B2 – 2019 awards FAQs
- B3 – 2019 awards – categories
- B4 – 2019 awards – best breastfeeding product
- B5 – 2019 awards – best feeding essential
- B6 – 2019 awards – vote
- M_B1 overview
- M_B2 Gold Elive Pump
- M_B3 Silver Medela Swing Maxi Flex
- M_B4 Bronze – Vital Baby Nurture Flexcone
- PB1 – 2019 awards – winners announced
- PB2 – 2019 winners
- PB3 – Elvie pump 2 – image only no text included on page

depending on the type of documents you have and how many there are, as can be seen in Box 11.4, where two contrasting approaches are shown.

Archival catalogues provide important information

If you are using documents from an online **archive**, you may find that it has a range of details for the documents available for you to download (usually as an Excel spreadsheet or csv. file). If so, this makes this section pretty easy for you: you need to download the information and decide which columns to include and exclude, or whether to aggregate the details across the **sample** for anonymity purposes. It may be that you include important details in a table in the methods or results chapter, but more comprehensive details as an appendix, so the examiner can return to the sources (if they are not already fully replicated) if they so wish. If not, you will need to create a table, database or spreadsheet containing the demographic details for your data set.

Box 11.3: Characteristics of note in samples of documents

- Known demographic characteristics of the **author**(s)
- Name of any organisation associated with the document
- The year of publication, and if this is substantiated or contested
- The intended audience and whether it is explicitly stated, or implied
- Word length

Box 11.4: Examples of sample descriptions and their location in the dissertation

In some pieces of research, sampling descriptions are provided in the introduction or the literature review; this is often when secondary analysis (a new analysis technique on documents that have been assessed before) is undertaken. An example of this is Anna Judson's (2020) paper, focusing on the role of scribes (those transcribing the words of others onto stone) in editing the contents of texts (see Chapter 12). She notes in the title that a particular set of documents – Linear B administrative documents from Mycenaean Greece – are chosen as the **sample** because there are already some known examples of scribes editing texts within the collection. The description of the **sample**'s contents does not need to be long, as it is referenced and described elsewhere.

By contrast, in Bennett and Kidd's (2017) research on British press descriptions of media studies education, they describe their **sample** in detail. Their core descriptor is the name of the newspaper. Alongside this, they include its type (**broadsheet** vs. **tabloid**) and its politics:

> The search produced 248 relevant articles from the main national British newspapers:
> - *The Guardian/Observer* (**broadsheet**, left of centre)
> - *Daily Express* (**tabloid**, right of centre)
> - *Daily Mail* (middle market **tabloid**, right of centre)
> (Bennett and Kidd, 2017: 166, my formatting)

What is the difference between coding and analysis?

Almost every type of qualitative analysis is structured around 'coding' data. In itself, coding is not linked to any one research paradigm or analysis strategy. Moreover, coding is not your full analysis, but one step within many analysis strategies, including content, thematic and **discourse analysis**, each of which relies on 'initial coding' to begin generating the content, themes or discourses within the data set. Johnny Saldaña's *The Coding Manual for Qualitative Researchers* shows, in considerable detail, practical examples of how to code that are accessible to novice researchers. For Saldaña, a code is 'most often a word or short phrase that symbolically assigns a summative, salient, essence-capturing, and/or evocative attribute for a portion of language-based or visual data' (Saldaña, 2015: 3). Codes can be *in vivo*, that is, taken verbatim from the data, or generated by the researcher in response to what they believe they have identified. There is no specific rule about the focus of codes, and they can centre around any number of actors or events. If you have yet to undertake any coding, it is definitely worth spending some time reviewing the 29 different approaches to coding that Saldaña identifies, each of which contains practical examples of coding data extracts.

How do I get started with my analysis?

Step 1 is definitely breathe. Don't panic: it will be OK. In this section I describe the practical steps to doing your analysis, whether electronically or on hard copies.

Preparing hard copy data

1. Never ever write on your original documents! Store these securely, if you are allowed to keep non-**anonymised** data.
2. If you need to anonymise the documents prior to analysis, you should:
   a. Make a copy of the data that is only printed on one side. Feel free to add page numbers, **DINs**, pseudonyms of **authors**, etc.
   b. Use a black permanent marker to cover up the details that need to be **anonymised** – you may wish to make notes as you go along, such as pseudonyms for people and places, or descriptors such as 'brother' or 'name of first school'.
   c. Photocopy this sheet again. Repeat until you cannot see any traces of the parts to be **anonymised.**
3. Scan copies of each sheet of data, so you have a full electronic back-up.
4. Securely dispose of (e.g.: shred) any copies with visible personal information you have created during the anonymisation process.

Using your planned analysis strategy

We discussed analysis strategies in Chapter 9, and you decided which strategy to follow before selecting your data. I recommended that you found a methods text describing the type of analysis that you wanted to do, so that you could clearly follow the steps.

1. Find guidance on your chosen analysis method.
2. Make notes on the steps that you will follow – these can be used in the analysis section of your methods chapter, as well as guiding you through the analysis.
3. Follow the guidance!
4. If you are struggling to get going with your analysis, or you are worried about the quality of the coding framework you have created, I recommend that you show your supervisor (or a peer using the same strategy).

Coding your data: a step within your analysis strategy

As mentioned above, coding is used in most qualitative analysis strategies. The way you code your data is always a variation of 'cut and paste' – you are aiming to show which sections fit within which codes. The way that you 'cut and paste' can include using hard copies of data, importing data into non-specialist software such as word processing programs, or within specialist qualitative analysis software. Regardless of *where* you undertake your analysis, the process is the same.

1. Get a full copy of your data set, either in hard copy, or within your chosen qualitative analysis software.
2. If you are coding 'by hand' on hard copies, get a range of highlighters, coloured pens or other ways to differentiate between codes when you are analysing your data.
3. Your analysis strategy will influence how you develop and use codes.
4. I find it helpful to have a list of codes printed out, or open on the side of my screen when I analyse my data.
5. If you are finding it difficult to use a single list of codes, you may wish to develop a hierarchy. For example, if I was looking at fashion, I could divide it into clothing, accessories, make-up and lifestyle. Within these, I could further subdivide, e.g. clothing could include shoes, dresses, coats, etc.
6. In the majority of analysis approaches, when coding, you should apply every code to each piece of data. This means if you develop codes as you are coding (an **inductive** approach, as advocated in Braun and Clarke, 2020), you should go back through your data to see if those codes could have been used earlier.

What should I include in my results chapter?

The analysis section was necessarily vague, as there are so many different approaches to documentary analysis. However, writing your results chapter generally follows a similar structure, with a large section in the middle dedicated to presenting your findings. Resource 11.1 provides a template for considering the contents of your results chapter; as always, check your dissertation handbook and dissertations in your department's library to see if this structure is best for you.

Reporting results vs discussion

Within your results chapter, it is usual in most disciplines (with exceptions in sociology, for example) to only report the findings of your analysis; interpretation of those findings in relation to literature takes place in the discussion. It can be difficult to understand where the boundary lies between reporting of findings and providing context. This is especially true when using an in-depth approach such as **discourse analysis**, where you are required to interpret the contents of the documents during analysis. If at all possible, find an example dissertation from your department that got a good grade and used a similar analysis approach to yours (again, remember to examine the structure, not content).

Introductory paragraph

As always, we say what we are going to say (then we say it, and then we say what we've said in the conclusion). The introductory paragraph will be a summary, so if you have used sub-headings, consider one sentence per sub-heading.

Description of data

Depending on your discipline, this may be in your methods chapter. If you do include it here, decide if you want to use a written description or a table. The purpose of this section is to help your examiner understand the boundaries of the data you have included. Any irregularities, such as most of your analysis coming from a minority of documents, should be reported here.

The main reporting of your findings

This section will use most of your word count for the chapter. You may choose to use a table or figure to display the interaction and any hierarchy between different parts of your findings, such as themes and sub-themes. It is common to include data extracts within your results chapter to give a flavour of the data that support your findings. Box 11.5 provides guidance on how to include quotations to best effect. However, it is important to note that it is almost always unnecessary to provide quotations for every point (in one journal article I had to do this, but it's not common – see Table 1 in Grant (2016a), which takes up four pages!); you are allowed to summarise points.

Resource 11.1: Structuring your results chapter

Section	Paragraph details/ purpose	Planned word count	Details
Introduction (1 paragraph)			
Description of data	Would a table or figure be helpful here?		NB: only if not included in your sampling section of the methods chapter
The main reporting of your analysis	Introduction to the qualitative analysis – one sentence per sub-heading		
	Sub-heading 1		
	Sub-heading 2		
	Sub-heading 3		
	Consider the use of a figure/table to show relationships		
Conclusion (1 paragraph)			Clearly state the main findings in relation to your research question

Sketch note 11.6: Do some writing today

> **Box 11.5: Including quotations or data extracts in your results chapter**
>
> Below are some pointers, to follow best practice.
>
> - If quotes are longer than a sentence (or a particular number of words, usually 40 words), they are usually taken out of the main text and indented. There will be guidance on this in your dissertation handbook as it varies by discipline.
> - Sometimes you will find a section of data with an excellent quote, then some irrelevant content, followed up with another excellent extract. Here it is possible to omit the irrelevant content, but to mark the quotation to show that this has occurred. Conventions include using ellipses '...', which can be enclosed in brackets '(...)' or '[...]'.
> - Sometimes **meaning** within quotations is only clear within the context of the full documents. For example, if somebody was writing about the decline of the red panda population, and part way through the document stated that 'their numbers have been in freefall ...' it would be acceptable to replace it with '[red panda] numbers have been in freefall' in your results chapter.

Summing up: the concluding paragraph

Here we are 'saying it again', providing a clear summary of the main findings, and signposting the **reader** to your discussion.

Conclusion

This chapter has focused on *how* to explain and report your sampling decisions coherently in your results chapter. We then considered practical tips to collecting and cataloguing your data, and how to report this within your results chapter if it is required. This was followed with the process of beginning your analysis, by preparing your full data set for analysis, using your planned analysis approach and learning how to 'code' your data, a step in most analysis strategies. Finally, tips have been provided in relation to the structure of your results chapter, and how to best include quotations. The next chapter of this book moves on to consider the quality of the data you are using and what to include in your discussion chapter.

Further reading

Undergraduate

Braun, V. and Clarke, V. (2013) *Successful Qualitative Research: A Practical Guide for Beginners*, London: SAGE, pp 178–274.

Yin, R.K. (2011) *Qualitative Research from Start to Finish*, London: The Guildford Press, pp 176–204.

Postgraduate

Braun, V. and Clarke, V. (2021) *Thematic Analysis: A Practical Guide*, London: SAGE.

Miles, M.B., Huberman, M. and Saldaña, J. (2013) *Qualitative Data Analysis: A Methods Sourcebook*, London: SAGE.

Saldaña, J. (2015) *The Coding Manual for Qualitative Researchers*, London: SAGE.

12

Assessing data quality and writing your discussion chapter

Summary

Within your discussion, you will be required to write a section identifying strengths and weaknesses of your research. Chapter 12 provides guidance to facilitate your assessment of quality and **biases** in your documents, which is slightly different from, for instance, studies using interviews. After this, we consider the other sections of your discussion chapter. These include comparing your results to your literature review and considering the implications of your research for society. Sometimes department procedure means that the dissertation ends with the discussion, while at other times a short concluding chapter is required. I discuss both approaches.

Objectives

By reading this chapter, you should understand:

- how to assess a document for signs of quality and **bias**;
- how to assess your findings against existing literature;
- what the implications of your research findings are for wider society;
- what to include in your discussion chapter.

Introduction: The importance of getting analytical

In Chapter 11, I mentioned that in your results chapter, you are supposed to present your analysis *without additional context*; the additional context is described within the discussion chapter. Along with your literature review, this is one of the main areas where you can present your own, original analytical thoughts. These are *essential* for obtaining a high grade. I did a (completely unscientific – it's lucky I'm not being graded!) search of the internet for marking schemes for dissertations, and selected elements relating to the discussion chapter from them. They included:

Sketch note 12.1: Think like an examiner

- analysed, argued, and reached conclusions that are informed by independent inquiry and other available information (University of Auckland, New Zealand, Maths);[1]
- independent and original thought (University of Bristol, UK, Deaf Studies);[2]
- comprehension and analysis of the issues involved (University of Nottingham, UK, Business School);[3]
- contribution to practice & research (National University of Singapore, Singapore, Business School);[4]
- critical evaluation (University of York, UK, Health Sciences).[5]

As you can see, the wording varies, and there may be particular elements that are emphasised within your department. You should review your dissertation handbook and marking scheme to see which skills are emphasised in your department (see also Chapter 3).

What does 'quality' and 'bias' mean in relation to documents?

A wide range of factors can fall within this sub-heading, including variation by the type of document that you use. Depending on whether new references can be introduced in your discussion chapter, you could include some references that relate to quality and **bias** issues in sources similar to yours; for example, defending the value of the type of document regardless of its faults. Below we examine legibility of handwritten documents, the *who, when and where* of authorship and how that may have caused **bias**, the intended audience and their likely understanding of the contents, and how this fits with the **authors**' intentions. There is an established literature on quality and **bias** within documents (e.g. Platt, 1981a, 1981b; Scott, 1990) that you may wish to consult.

The presence or absence of legibility and clarity of meaning

When using handwritten data or damaged or incomplete (partial) documents, establishing what the document 'said' can be challenging. Furthermore, when collecting historical data from **archives** or elsewhere, the handwriting can be very difficult to decipher. Within interview-based research, it is widely accepted that transcription is a core component of analysis (e.g. Braun and Clarke, 2013), allowing the researcher to become familiar with the data. However, transcription of longer pieces of spoken or handwritten words is *never* a neutral act creating a single 'truth'; there may be sections where it is impossible to understand words or phrases, misunderstandings may occur between the original data and the transcript, and incorrect assumptions may be made. When using archival data, you may find a transcript, or a detailed account of the document created by an **archivist**; it is important to remember that these documents have also been constructed, with their own quality and **bias** issues.

By contrast, when we undertake documentary analysis in the twenty-first century, our data mostly come neatly word processed. This has advantages in terms of saving time, but handwritten documents leave interesting clues for us about **meaning**. For example, handwritten notes posted in communal kitchens are absolutely fascinating (some words larger than others, in capitals or underlined multiple times), allowing us to interpret energy and emphasis more easily than in a typed document (see sketch note 12.2).

Who wrote the document; why, when and where?

Alongside legibility, we should consider the intended **meaning** and purpose of the documents. Individuals have a wide range of motivations for writing. For example, sometimes people are paid to undertake writing (e.g. journalists,

Sketch note 12.2: An example of a note to fellow kitchen users

political advisers or marketers). Others may write without payment because they feel strongly about an issue of social justice, or they wish to resist an unequal and hateful society. Less controversially, at the time of writing, it was very common for individuals to hold social media accounts to promote their work or just their lifestyle. With the advent of interactive social media, we can also readily find examples of people in overlapping categories, known as 'influencers'.

We can understand the relationship between **meaning** and purpose through considering who the **authors** were, and the reason they created the document. At undergraduate level, I would expect to see some background information on who the person or organisation was, and suspected **biases**. For example, when considering documents from businesses, an important point to consider is that the purpose of a business is to make money, and the words and images used may have alternative **meanings** (see Ball (2010) for an example).

The *when* and *where* of document creation are also relevant. This means considering the geo–political context and its impact on the documents included. For example, things that were not allowed within an organisation, or were illegal, would have been unlikely to be included (see Grant, 2021). Likewise, the language used, and the **meaning** conveyed by certain words and phrases changes over time. If you have undertaken a **discourse analysis**, you have already done some of this thinking; if not, a sentence or two on the context should appear in your discussion.

Who is the intended audience?

We should also consider the intended **reader**. When **authors** are creating documents, they (and their **editors** or employers) will have thought about their intended audience. Are there any clues within the document, or the **archive** from which it came, that indicate who the **author** believed would be the primary audience? For example, you may consider the formality of the language used, how easy or difficult the text is to read (because of length of sentence and individual words). Individuals undertake image management constantly, which Goffman (1959) describes in detail. For example, think about how you might write to a partner or close friend, and contrast that with how you would write to a politician on an issue you find important. Very few people present the same version of themselves at all times. In relation to the analysis of documents, the intended **reader** becomes important as we consider whether this is a space in which the **author** felt they could be open and vulnerable. On social media, many users present an idealised version of themselves and their lives (see, for example, Grant and O'Mahoney, 2016).

How does it compare to similar documents?

Scott (1990: 19) describes this as '**representativeness**'. While we talked in Part II about choosing documents to fit your **research question**, that was a

Sketch note 12.3: Representativeness matters

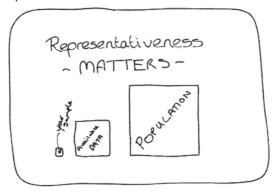

practical form of sampling, based on the documents available. To consider the **population** of documents as a whole, however, we need to think about every document that could answer your **research question**, the proportion available to you and, from that, the **sample** you collected and analysed (see sketch note 12.3). For your dissertation we don't need to consider this too deeply (it will likely be one or two sentences), but you do need to make a statement about how **representative** your **sample** was.

How do I assess my data for quality and bias?

Resource 12.1 provides a template that you can use in your own research to examine legibility, authorship, purpose, context and fit with the **population** of documents. You may wish to use multiple copies (one per document or set of documents) if you need to carry out an in-depth analysis of the **biases** within your **sample**. In an undergraduate dissertation, you will only need a few paragraphs on the strengths and weaknesses of your dissertation as a whole, and this should be reflected in how much time you spend on this. I provide a worked example below, in relation to my experience as a journalistic **author**.

So, on to considering the **biases** relating to the purpose and context in my own writing for *The Conversation*, an online news site run by a group of international universities. First, considering the purpose, the aim of *The Conversation* is to disseminate academic research. However, if you think back to Chapter 3, we're currently in a neoliberal period with reduced government funding. Accordingly, we could suggest that *The Conversation* has been set up to highlight the value of academic research for society. In terms of my motivation, I told the **editor**, when publishing articles on infant feeding and the bullying of mothers in public, that my core aim was to transmit the message 'stop being mean to mums'. However, that was the message rather than my only *motivation* for working for free (**authors** don't get paid to write for *The Conversation*). My motivation for writing was to enhance my career. **Editors** are in a relatively stronger position than writers, for example writing headlines for **journalists** in some instances. Like scribes

Resource 12.1: Considering quality and bias in documents

Document name/number

Is it fully legible? (damaged; incomplete; forgery; handwriting)

Who is the author? (Background e.g.: age, gender, ethnicity, etc.; use of multiple authors; name of an organisation or group who employs author; use of editors)

What was the purpose? (Intended audience; stated purpose; factors influencing purpose (including money); **credibility**; ulterior motive; multiple purposes)

When and where was the context? (Creation and planned consumption of document; legality, breaking rules, morality and secrets; alternative meanings for content (subtle/overt))

How does it compare to other documents in your population? (Contents of FULL population; contents of available population; contents of your sample)

Other

in times past (Judson, 2020), this can have a big impact on the **meaning** being transmitted due to the exclusion or amendment of content. Fortunately, my **editor** only edited my draft using an online platform, to ensure it met a reading age suitable for 10–year–olds. This changed the language used and the complexity of the argument in places.

What should I include in my discussion chapter?

I've spent a lot of time discussing quality and **bias** within documentary data because it is quite different from other forms of data. However, as noted, it is only likely to be one to three paragraphs long in the average undergraduate dissertation. That brings us nicely onto what most dissertations *will* contain in their discussion chapter, which I show in Resource 12.2. As always, your department may have a different way of looking at things, so do look at your dissertation handbook and examples of good dissertations in your department.

Overview of results

This is generally one paragraph. The first sentence can rephrase the **research question**, such as 'This study aimed to (xyz)'. To help you write the summary, you can look at the summary of results that you prepared for the first paragraph of your results chapter. Don't repeat it word for word, but you can use that and/or the headings from your results chapter as a starting point.

Comparing your results to existing literature

Doing the work to get to this point can take time and thought. Chapter 7 described one approach to the literature review as funnelling the **reader** from broad concepts to the research that is most similar to your dissertation. This section can be similar in structure, starting out by comparing your research to the existing literature in general terms, without too much information. From here, you can move to comparing your research to the most similar pieces of research, found toward the end of your literature review. You can highlight differences in your **sample** of documents and any corresponding differences in findings. At the end of this section, you can report any novel findings that have come from your study, if applicable.

Understanding the limitations of your research

At the beginning of this chapter, we considered quality and **biases** within your **sample**. Alongside sampling decisions, you should comment on the appropriateness of your whole research design, including using documents as data, and the analysis approach you adopted. You can choose to make a statement that,

Resource 12.2: Structuring your discussion chapter

Section	Paragraph details/ purpose	Planned word count	Details
Introduction (1 paragraph)			
Overview of findings (1 paragraph)			
Comparing your results to existing literature	If you use headings in this section, write a brief introduction before the first heading		
	Sub-heading 1		
	Sub-heading 2		
	Sub-heading 3		
Strengths and limitations			
Implications for future research, policy and practice			
Conclusion (1 paragraph)			Clearly state the main conclusion of your research in relation to existing literature, policy or practice. **NB: Conclusions must be **justifiable****

with hindsight having completed the project, an alternative approach (which you name) may have been more appropriate.

Implications for future research, policy and practice

This section will vary by discipline – you can get an idea of what might go in this section based on the information included in your introduction, that is, what made your research important. If you mention any laws or policies in your introduction, refer back to them; what does your research mean in relation to the law or policy? Practice refers to academic disciplines which overlap with occupational groups; for example, in relation to healthcare, education, housing, welfare and social services. Finally, based on everything you've covered in your discussion, what would your recommendation be for further research in the area?

Concluding sections

Depending on the norms within your department, you may be required to write a separate conclusion chapter, which is usually a page or two long. Alternatively, some departments use a single paragraph at the end of the discussion – usually beginning 'To conclude …' or 'In conclusion …' – as the final written part, ahead of the references section. You can check your dissertation handbook and copies of dissertations from your department, and ask your supervisor which approach you should take; this will have some implications for the word length of your discussion, as a single paragraph will be around 250 words, but a separate chapter may be up to 1,000 or more within master's and doctoral dissertations. The conclusions that you draw *must* be justifiable in the context of the limitations of your research. That means that if you did a piece of research on a collection of magazines focused on collecting antiques made of metal, all of which came from the UK, it would *only* be appropriate to draw conclusions that relate to British metallic antiques magazines from the period of your **sample**. Claiming that your research had implications for *all* magazines, or even all antiques magazines, would be unsubstantiated. As one of the last things that your examiner is going to read, making unreasonable claims of influence can have a negative impact on their assessment of your analytical skill.

Conclusion

This chapter has focused on the skills and contents required in your discussion chapter. First, we considered in detail how to assess quality and **bias** within your **sample** of documents, a component of the strengths and weaknesses section of your discussion. From here, I gave an example of the **biases** within my own journalistic writing and outlined a structure that it might be helpful for you to follow. The second section of the chapter outlined a structure and overview of the contents of your discussion chapter. As always, there are differences by discipline and department as to what is included; this means that sometimes dissertations end with the discussion, including a concluding paragraph. Other times, a separate conclusion chapter is used. In the final substantive chapter of this book, we put together all your research and writing into the full dissertation.

Further reading

Undergraduate

Largan, C. and Morris, T. (2019) *Qualitative Secondary Research: A Step-by-step Guide*, London: SAGE, pp 277–300.

Prior, L. (2003) *Using Documents in Social Research*, London: SAGE, pp 107–124.

Scott, J. (1990) *A Matter of Record: Documentary Sources in Social Research*, London: John Wiley & Sons, pp 19–35.

Postgraduate

Grant, A. (2019) *Doing Excellent Social Research with Documents: Practical Examples and Guidance for Qualitative Researchers*, Abingdon: Routledge.

Prior, L. (2003) *Using Documents in Social Research*, London: SAGE.

Scott, J. (1990) *A Matter of Record: Documentary Sources in Social Research*, London: John Wiley & Sons.

Creating the final dissertation

Summary

Chapter 13 is the last of our main chapters (like some dissertations, I have a brief concluding chapter coming up after this). In it, we go from your research diary, notes, completed resources and draft chapters to finishing off your dissertation. I describe ways to get yourself in the 'zone' of writing, to boost your word count if you have been struggling. Following this, I return to relationships with your supervisor, and incorporating their feedback into your work. This is often challenging and upsetting, but remember it is not personal. From not having enough words, you will likely end up at a point where you have too many words, and I help you to think about how best to stay within your word count. Once the writing is over, it is time for the fiddly bits of formatting, including 'front matter' such as declarations that the work is your own, and appendices, such as copies of some of your data or an extract from your analysis. The final step before submission is proofreading, and I'll give you a few hints.

Objectives

By reading this chapter, you should understand:

- that there is no 'right' way to write;
- how to incorporate your supervisor's feedback;
- the need for 'front matter' and appendices;
- how to go about editing and proofreading.

Introduction: How can I get words on the page quickly?

My plan for this section is to help you get words on paper (or screen); editing comes later. This is often the most difficult part for students, who can find a lot of innovative ways to procrastinate! They have enthusiasm when it comes to collecting data and can excitedly tell me what they have found during their analysis. If you feel like this, all the information that needs to be written down is already in your head. I hope this is a relief, although I imagine some of you are thinking 'but you really don't know how bad I am at writing'. Like many things in life, writing is a skill that improves with time; you are not expected to be experts at writing at your career stage. So, it is important to do *something* about getting words on the page. I like the approach of having to stay at my desk for a certain amount of time writing *something*; even if that something is that I don't know anything about a topic. That just means that when I come back to review my notes, I know that I need to do some reading. In Box 13.1, I include my top tips for getting words on the page quickly.

> ### Box 13.1: How to quickly get words on the page – Aimee's approach
>
> - Wear comfortable clothes.
> - Go to the toilet, get a drink, eat a snack if you are hungry (but do not procrastinate cooking elaborate food).
> - Put your phone on silent and tell anybody at home not to disturb you unless it's very important.
> - Sit (or stand) where you feel most comfortable writing. This can be at a desk, but also on your sofa, in bed or at your kitchen worktop if you don't have a standing desk and want to stand to write.
> - Write for at least 30 minutes without leaving your space. It doesn't matter if you are writing 'insert a sentence about the relationship between X and Y here'.
> - Before leaving your writing space, and this is *crucial* to your ongoing success, add some notes about what you *will* (no excuses) write about tomorrow.

Many students will be disabled in some way or may have caring responsibilities or a job. Flexibility is necessary for them to fit in blocks of writing time. In this case, they may feel that they are 'doing it wrong'. I'll let you into a secret: many academics are secretive about how they write, also thinking that they are doing it 'wrong'. As long as you get some words on the page, it doesn't matter what your process is. In Box 13.2, I share my writing ritual.

> ### Box 13.2: Changes to Aimee's writing ritual over time
>
> Book number one (Grant, 2019) was written when I wasn't in brilliant health but was 'soldiering on' before I got very unwell. My ritual was solid, and I rarely took a day off. First thing in the morning, before getting dressed (i.e. still in my PJs), I put the kettle on, went to the toilet, made a lemon and ginger tea and then went to my desk. I closed the door,

which my husband knew meant 'do not disturb unless you are seriously bleeding or otherwise at risk of death'. I like to have a blanket over my legs as I write, so there is always one on my desk chair. Slippers are a must, as cold feet distract me. By contrast, I wrote a lot of my PhD (which I worked on from 2007 to 2011) in bed, as I recovered from a debilitating period of Chronic Fatigue Syndrome, and then it became my habit – the most productive place for me to work from, as I could spread books and journal articles around me on the king-size bed and have the one I needed immediately to hand.

This book was written more slowly; an idea that slowly came to fruition, starting with an idea in 2017, and interrupted by significant new disabilities, miscarriages and bereavement. Since my PhD I have developed a bad back, so writing in bed when I have fatigue is no longer suitable (it would also bother my husband to sweep aside a sea of papers each night!). I am often stiff and sore in the mornings, as I suffer from fibromyalgia, so there is now an orthopaedic desk chair with an electric heating pad on the back of it to ease my pain as I write (and an incentive to stay at my desk). Unlike before, I don't have a fixed writing time and do not have set days, but when I feel that I can write, I do. This time, I sit at my desk and work in long bursts of time; being Autistic and having hyperfocus is *very* helpful when you are a researcher (see Grant and Kara, 2021)! This is *absolutely not* the recommended way of working in most 'how to write' guides, but there will be other people who prefer this approach or need to use it because of factors beyond their control. It is not as reliable as getting into a routine, but it can work.

Sketch note 13.1: Do some writing today

How do I incorporate my supervisor's feedback?

I'm hoping that most of you feel OK with receiving feedback after reading Chapter 4. For those of you who don't, it would be helpful for you to think about what the issue is before continuing. Your draft chapters with supervisor's comments are *literally* documents, and we know how troublesome they can be! Below I take you through some common issues.

Help! I can't understand what they mean

This can fall into two camps. First, considering legibility. If your supervisor is writing on your work by hand – something I sometimes choose to do – can you read their writing? If not, you need to speak up. In my supervisions, I got my supervisor to go through his handwritten comments and made notes as he spoke, as at times his writing was very difficult to read. If it's not possible to have a meeting with them, you could send scans (I use the Adobe Scan app on my phone) of the page to them, with the section you can't read highlighted. I would try to look through all the chapters reviewed together and send them in one go if possible. Second, thinking about **meaning** in documents, we know that what the **author** intended to mean might not be what the intended audience understands when they consume it. If you are not sure what they mean, or what they intend you to do with their comment, I would advise you to ask.

The comments are all negative; I'm really demoralised

This is a frequent complaint I've heard from students I am not supervising. Sometimes students take a lack of positive comments as a sign of their work being poor. If you receive good feedback face-to-face, it is likely that your supervisor is choosing to only highlight things they think you need to consider further. If it has upset you, first consider writing in your research diary and speaking to

Sketch note 13.2: Don't forget to use your research diary

Sketch note 13.3: Don't panic: plan!

peers. If you are unable to shake your concerns, ask your supervisor if they have any worries about the standard of your work, or if they think you might fail. This will give you either the reassurance that you need or will give you valuable pointers for things that need improvement.

There are so many comments, I don't have time to address them!

If you are running out of time and not eligible for an extension, I suggest that you take each of your draft chapters and divide them into those that have been reviewed and revised by you, and those that have not. Those that have not been revised at all may need the most attention, although only you can tell based on your supervisor's comments. I suggest making a plan – count each day or block of a few hours that you have remaining and make a list of comments that could not be dealt with in five minutes. Decide which ones are most important.

How do I create a full draft dissertation?

Step 1: Gather all of your work

Hopefully as you've been reading, you have used some of the downloadable resources, written your research diary and drafted some chapters. If you haven't, you can still go back to the relevant chapters to learn from the resources if you feel stuck. If you're ready to jump into pulling together your final dissertation, I strongly recommend that you pool EVERYTHING THAT YOU HAVE WRITTEN; start a new folder and put the most up-to-date version of each thing in that folder. If you have versions of chapters in your emails with your supervisor's comments, make sure they are included.

Sketch note 13.4: Be methodical and organised

Step 2: Examine each individual chapter for completeness

At this point, you are seeing if you have:

- included an introduction, saying what you are going to say;
- followed a logical structure (see the guidance in the relevant chapter of this book, your dissertation handbook and completed dissertations from your department);
- balanced the sections within your chapter, so they are roughly even; if not, should the structure be amended?
- finished with a conclusion that signposts to the next chapter;
- reviewed and amended the chapter based on feedback from your supervisor;
- completed each section; if not, think about what you need to include and do it;
- tidied up any tables, boxes or figures, including giving them a title and any footnotes required;
- referenced everywhere that it's needed.

I use comment bubbles or notes in bold with highlighting to alert me to sections that need attention; you may choose to use this approach. I also find that at a certain stage it becomes useful to print out the entire document, but this may or may not help you.

Step 3: Ensure you are ethical in your dissertation

Data mining is the name given to going onto the internet and downloading (often a large volume of) information for the purposes of conducting research. It is traditionally associated with more quantitative approaches; for example, mining

Sketch note 13.5: Don't forget to be ethical

Twitter and then analysing the data using high-powered computers and a pre-determined list of positive or negative words. In this type of research, people's personal information, including large extracts of their original wording, is rarely reported.

By contrast, I have used data mining in my analysis, but undertaken a more qualitative approach where I consider discourses and unspoken **meaning**s (see, for example, Grant, 2016b). I have also collected and analysed images used on social media posts. However, to ensure my data mining is ethical, I have not repeated words **verbatim**, and I have not reproduced any images. Instead, I have 'minimally altered' **authors'** words, by correcting spelling mistakes, substituting a word for a very similar word, and changing or removing names of individuals or places. For an example of minimally altering data, see Box 13.3.

Step 4: Creating the actual dissertation

In this stage, all your chapters, tables and figures are combined into one document. A few points for you to consider are:

- This can be a time when word processing software is not completely reliable, although this has improved throughout the years. Consider adjusting your settings so that your 'auto-save' function occurs every few minutes. Also, save your work regularly.
- Take a copy of each of your chapters and paste it into the document. If you have used referencing software, it may be slow to paste. Do not cut the original; ensure you retain a copy, in case your software crashes.

Box 13.3: Minimally altering data to protect anonymity

If I were undertaking research on students' views of doing their dissertation, I could mine a social media site, such as Instagram, for data. Suppose I found an Instagram post that had a photo of the student doing a 'sad but beautiful' face accompanied with the following text:

So bored writing my dissertation for Aimee Grant's class right now – please send nachos and chocolate to #Cardiff.

There would be a lot of ways in which the student could be identified; their image in the photograph, naming me as their dissertation supervisor, and using a hashtag to highlight the geographic location/university. Because of this, I could not ethically repeat the image or text as data. However, if it was a particularly good quote that I really wanted to include, one solution would be to minimally alter it to maintain anonymity and privacy, to:

So bored writing my (report) for (my tutor's) class right now – please send nachos and chocolate to #(City in the UK).

Standard anonymity rules would remove the names of the tutor and the location. In addition, I changed dissertation to '(report)'. I could also have changed 'nachos and chocolate' to 'crisps and cake'; the individual items would have changed, but I would have retained the fact that two distinct food items were requested, one savoury and the other sweet. Furthermore, needing chocolate is something frequently used as a marker of feminine exasperation ('ugh, I really need chocolate!'), and cake is used in a similar way.

This is the approach that I suggest my students use, but your dissertation supervisor may have alternative ideas. It is best to discuss this with them before writing up.

- Once all of the chapters are in, combine the references for the entire dissertation; if you have used software to reference, you should 'refresh' it to combine them.
- You should use a consistent font and font size throughout (except for headings) to make the dissertation look coherent.
- Headings help your examiner to follow what is important in each chapter. You can use headings, sub–headings, and sub–sub–headings. It is not usual to include more than three layers of headings (excluding the title of the chapter), so if you find yourself going beyond three levels of heading, consider whether

you need to change the structure – this does not need to include large changes to the contents.

- Similarly, if you do not have many headings within the body of your chapter, it will be difficult for your examiner to read.
- You will almost certainly need a table of contents as part of your front matter, and one way to generate this is to use the built-in headings on your word processing software (I use Microsoft Word), and then to auto-generate the table. Doing so will enable you to check the headings are at the intended level.

Step 5: Writing your abstract

At this stage in your academic journey, you are likely to have read hundreds of abstracts, but may not have needed to write one before. A few tips:

- Abstracts have a strict word limit; don't be tempted to go over it.
- Abstracts can be either structured (containing headings) or unstructured (one long paragraph). It is important to find out which format you need to use.
- The abstract should be a chronological journey through your dissertation.

Consider your word count carefully and write the following:

1. one sentence – why is your topic area important?
2. a sentence or two on your literature review;
3. one sentence – what is your **research question**? For example, 'this research asks why (x, y, z) …';
4. a few sentences on your methods, including the data used and the analysis approach;
5. a few sentences on your results, highlighting the key findings;
6. a sentence or two on your discussion; how has this project moved the body of literature on?
7. a concluding sentence to either say that you will outline the implications of your research for research/policy/practice, or state a very definitive conclusion, if you have arrived at one.

Step 6: Include 'front matter' and appendices

In your dissertation module handbook, the required front matter and appendices will be outlined. In most departments, you will be required to include the following:

- a title page, stating your name, the title of the dissertation, the name of your university and the degree that you are submitting it for;

- a page of declarations, often requiring a signature, stating that you have not submitted it for another degree previously and that it is all your own work except for sources you have referenced;
- a contents page, with page numbers referring to the beginning of each chapter.

As well as front matter, appendices may be used. These are often data collection tools, data or examples of analysis. In my experience, it is not usual to submit a full data set as an appendix with your dissertation. Again, consult your dissertation handbook for guidance.

The final bit: editing and proofreading

There is not a standard definition of what editing is; its purpose varies depending on the type of document, the **author** and the intended **readers**. In terms of your dissertation, I present some common types of editing that may be required, before considering proofreading.

Editing

Earlier in the chapter, we spoke about incorporating your supervisor's comments, and it can be tempting to think that that is the only type of editing required. However, if you are aiming for the best grade possible, it is sensible to review your full draft, as your writing style and ability will change over time. Editing will take time and is more challenging if it is rushed. Here are some things to consider:

- Are there sentences or paragraphs that are unclear?
- Are there sentences that are so long they are confusing?
- Are any of your paragraphs longer than 16 lines? If so, can it be split into two paragraphs?
- Are there any sections that talk at length about something that could be said very concisely?
- Does each chapter's introduction make the chapter sound interesting and/or important?
- Do the headings in your chapters sound like they belong together (are they in the same style)?
- Do you use jargon, or long or complex words, aiming to sound clever? If so, I suggest changing the language, so it is easier to read.
- Are there any terms you have to use which your examiner may not understand? If so, add a footnote the first time you use it, giving a definition.

I find it helpful to check if I am clear and consistent by reading my work aloud.

Proofreading

Some examiners are *very* picky when it comes to typos, as well as more serious errors. For example, following my PhD viva (the oral exam), one of my examiners handed me a copy of my dissertation in which he had folded over the corner of each page where there was a spelling mistake; there were a lot of folded corners! My thesis had been professionally proofread (because I'm Dyslexic), but clearly by someone who wasn't very good at their job! It is sensible to use a spellchecker at a minimum. If you know that spelling and grammar are not your strong points, then this is absolutely no reflection of your intellectual capacity. Do not be embarrassed but try to find a solution; I have included some suggestions in Box 13.4.

Box 13.4: A note on spelling, punctuation and grammar

Supervisory review of your written work does *not* routinely include reviewing your work for typographical errors (spelling mistakes, etc.). If you suspect that you may be dyslexic or have a similar neurodiversity or specific learning disability, get in touch with your student support centre and find out how you can access support for Disabled students, including potentially proofreading of your dissertation. If these issues are challenging simply because you were not taught these things at school, you may benefit from using applications or software that will check your grammar for you or allow your document to be read aloud to you, so that you can more easily identify issues. I use the (free version of the) Grammarly extension, alongside the inbuilt spelling and grammar check within my word processing software. Finally, due to my dyslexia, I dictate much of my 'written' work using a program called Dragon and another called Claro Read that reads my written words aloud.

Reviewing your references

As well as proofreading your text, you should proofread your references; this means checking that each reference in the main text is included in the reference list at the end. Also, there should not be any sources in the reference list that are not included in your chapters. Furthermore, you should check the spelling of names and the format of dates.

Conclusion

This chapter has focused on the final push toward completing your dissertation. First, we considered how to get words on the page. Following this, we looked at

Sketch note 13.6: Be proud you finished your dissertation!

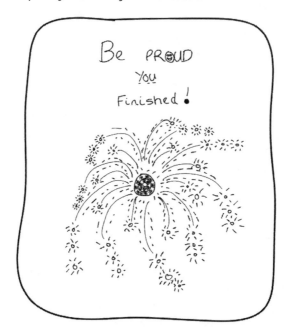

ways that it can be challenging to respond to your supervisor's feedback. I then provided guidance on bringing together all of the writing that you have created, then adding an abstract, front matter and appendices. Finally, we considered editing and proofreading the document as a whole; a task that can take some time, but enhances clarity. In the next chapter, I say a brief goodbye to you all. Thank you for allowing me to join you on your dissertation journey.

Further reading

Undergraduate

Bell, J. and Waters, S. (2014) *Doing Your Research Project: A Guide for First-time Researchers*, New York: Open University Press, pp 256–273.

Boyle, P. (2010) *Demystifying Dissertation Writing: A Streamlined Process from Choice of Topic to Final Text*, Sterling, VG: Stylus, pp 165–178.

Postgraduate

Billingham, J. (2002) *Editing and Revising Text*, Oxford: Oxford University Press.

Boyle, P. (2010) *Demystifying Dissertation Writing: A Streamlined Process from Choice of Topic to Final Text*, Sterling, VG: Stylus.

Gardiner, M. and Kearns, H. (2010) *Turbocharge Your Writing*, Adelaide: Flinders Press.

14

Concluding remarks

It has absolutely been my pleasure writing this book. In academia, it is very rare to get the chance to write without large amounts of challenging reading, and frequent citations as you write: like many of you **readers**, I don't love referencing!

Doing Your Research Project with Documents aimed to enable students completing a dissertation using documents as data to better understand both the process of undertaking research with documents, and how to write their dissertation. I presented the process in three stages: *Getting going, Making decisions*, and *Getting it done*! I hope that you have found this structure accessible and useful in your work, even though your work is likely to have gone off this faux-linear path. Furthermore, if you have followed the book through each chapter, the small pieces of writing that you have regularly done in response to the resources will add up to a useful foundation for your dissertation. There will hopefully also be some useful content to contribute toward each chapter in your research diary. If you haven't completed these as you've gone through the process, you can still benefit by going to the resources in each chapter and seeing if any can provide retrospective clarity.

My hope was to write a book that meant that students – especially those from marginalised backgrounds – would find their dissertation less daunting. If you have enjoyed undertaking your dissertation, you may wish to continue your studies, undertaking a postgraduate taught or research degree. In general, if you achieve a 2:1 in your dissertation, you are considered capable to progress (although sometimes marking is undertaken by those who have **epistemological** differences to you, so a low mark does not always mean a poor piece of research). That said, there are often significant financial costs associated with undertaking postgraduate study, and you should bear in mind the likely employment prospects (if that is your aim for further study) before embarking on a master's or doctorate. You may also find it useful to engage with Clark and Sousa's (2018) *How to Be a Happy Academic* before you become an unhappy academic!

As always, I am very happy to receive feedback – positive and negative – to help me understand how to better support **readers** in future editions and students that I personally support through their dissertations. The easiest way to contact me is via Twitter; I am @DrAimeeGrant.

Glossary

This list provides an overview of the more specialist terms used in the book. For further information, you can refer to this section of the book by finding the same term within the index. More detailed information can be found within sources that I have signposted you to, or by discussing with your dissertation supervisor.

Actor Network Theory	A **theory** that explains how human 'actors' are influenced by non-human 'actors', resulting in particular behaviours.
Anonymised	Data WILL be altered, such as removing names and places, so that nobody can tell who provided them. Commonly within research studies, anonyzmity will be promised to participants.
Anonymity	Ensuring that outputs from research do not contain details that could lead to participants being identified.
Archive(s)	A collection of documents, often historical.
Archivist(s)	A specialist worker in an **archive**, who collects new documents and preserves, organises, and arranges access to existing documents in the **archive**.
ATLAS.ti	A computer program that facilitates coding and retrieval of qualitative data (see also **CAQDAS**).
Authenticity	A document is authentic when it is an original or a complete copy.
Author(s)	An individual or group of people who have written a document.
Bias(es)	Anything that changes the results of a research project. This can include issues with the researcher, with data, and within the analysis.
Bloggers	Individuals who create an online diary or journal, known as a blog.

Blog(s)	An online 'weblog', akin to a diary or journal.
Boolean operators	A way of combining or excluding keywords in a search of a database. Commonly used **Boolean operators** include AND, OR and NOT.
Broadsheet (newspapers)	Traditionally **broadsheets** would have been printed on larger paper than **tabloid** newspapers; the content also varies in that **broadsheets** are generally more serious.
CAQDAS	The abbreviation given to Computer Assisted Qualitative Data Analysis Software, including **ATLAS.ti** and **NVivo**. These programs contain specific tools to enable researchers to code data and retrieve their coding.
Coding framework	A document that includes all of the codes to be used in data analysis. This may be finalised before analysis begins (deductive analysis) or created during analysis (inductive analysis).
Content analysis	An analysis strategy that requires the researcher to develop a coding framework linked to the **research question** and used to code all data sources. See Table 9.1.
Credibility	A document has high levels of **credibility** when an **author** reports their sincere views of events.
Deductive	A way of reasoning where data are used to test an existing **theory**. In qualitative research this often involves using pre-defined codes to analyse data (the opposite of **inductive** reasoning).
Discourse analysis	A way of critically analysing data in order to understand language and power.
Document Identification Number (DIN)	A unique identification number given to each document in a **sample**, to allow for ease of retrieval and to ensure any data loss is easily identifiable.

Double coding	The practice of a piece of analysis being undertaken independently by two researchers, to compare the similarity of their findings. Double coding is commonly found within positivist research paradigms.
Editor(s)	An individual who has overall responsibility for a piece of writing and may make changes to its content and **meaning**.
Epistemology/ epistemologies	A **theory** of how knowledge is created and its **validity**.
Ethical approval	Is given to research protocols once they have been reviewed by a **research ethics committee** and deemed to be ethically appropriate.
Ethnography	A form of qualitative inquiry that uses a range of methods, such as observation, interviews and analysis of documents, to understand a phenomenon.
Gantt chart	A graphical representation of a project timetable (see, for example, Resource 3.3). Time is usually displayed in the columns, with tasks represented by rows; shading is used to highlight the time when the task should occur.
Hand coding	The practice of conducting qualitative data analysis on hard copies of data, making annotations in margins and highlighting relevant sections of the data. Hand coding is in contrast to computer-asssisted qualitative analysis.
Inductive	An approach to research which allows new theories and themes to emerge 'from the data', although this will be affected by the researcher's existing knowledge and experiences.
Interpretivist	An approach to studying society which assumes that there is no single 'truth', and that scientific enquiry must include interpretation.

Keywords	A list of topics, research fields and methods that is found on most journal articles, to help people identify relevant articles when searching in academic databases.
Meaning	Whether the document can be easily read, and if the impact of the social context on content can be deciphered.
Nexis®	A database for the storage and retrieval of news media articles.
NVivo	A **CAQDAS** program to facilitate qualitative data analysis.
Ontology/ontologies	A range of approaches to understanding reality.
Piloting	The practice of testing out research procedures, for example, an analysis strategy, prior to formally beginning undertaking the research activity.
Population	All of the documents that could answer your **research question** (including those that you may not be able to access).
Positionality	All researchers have a positionality, which relates to their demographics, identity and social positions. The consideration of the impact of positionality on research is known as **reflexivity**.
Positivist	An approach to studying society which assumes that a certain 'truth' can be found through rigorous scientific enquiry. An alternative **ontology** is **social constructionism**.
Postcards	A card for sending a message to somebody by post, usually 6" by 4" in size, with a photograph or image on the front.
Rapport	The degree of comfort achieved between a researcher and research participants. Commonly considered within qualitative research.

Reader(s)	Somebody who is consuming a document in some way.
Reflexive Thematic Analysis	A form of qualitative thematic analysis associated with Virginia Braun and Victoria Clarke (see for example: 2019; 2020; 2021).
Reflexivity	The process of critically considering one's own effect on the research. Sometimes also referred to as positionality.
Representativeness	A reference to whether the data have been selected using probability sampling or purposive sampling. Missing data can also affect how **representative** a **sample** is.
Research ethics committee	A group of people affiliated to an organisation who review protocols for research projects to ensure that they are ethically appropriate.
Research paradigms	A set of beliefs based on assumptions related to ontology and epistemology.
Research question(s)	A pre-defined question which a research project will attempt to answer.
Rigour	An assessment of the quality of research design and processes. The definition of **rigour** varies between qualitative and quantitative inquiry.
Sample	The documents you include in your analysis.
Semiotics/semiotic analysis	The study of signs and signifiers and how they crate shared meanings between authors and readers.
Social constructionism	An approach to studying society that does not assume the existence of a single 'true' reality. Instead realities are believed to be constructed between the individuals using language and actions.

Tabloid (newspapers)	These are smaller in size than **broadsheet** newspapers. The content is often less serious and focused on sensationalising crime and celebrity gossip.
Thematic analysis	An analysis strategy that involves either **inductively** or **deductively** identifying themes, and coding data for these themes, to allow a comparison across the data set. See Chapter 9.
Theory	A statement about how and/or why things occur in society.
Triangulation	A way of combining two or more sets of data in order to gain a greater understanding of a phenomenon.
Validity	The extent to which a research project is able to answer its **research question**.
Verbatim	The practice of recording somebody's exact words.
Visual or creative methods	A qualitative research strategy which uses visual materials or creative tasks to co-produce data with participants.

Notes

Chapter 3

[1] https://en.wikipedia.org/wiki/List_of_suicide_crisis_lines [Accessed 27 March 2021]

Chapter 6

[1] https://en.wikipedia.org/wiki/List_of_suicide_crisis_lines [Accessed 27 March 2021]

Chapter 13

[1] https://cdn.auckland.ac.nz/assets/math/for/current-students/documents/MSc-Marking-Guidelines.pdf [Accessed 20 February 2021]

[2] www.bris.ac.uk/Depts/DeafStudiesTeaching/dissert/Marking%20Scheme.htm [Accessed 20 February 2021]

[3] www.nottingham.ac.uk/academicservices/documents/qmdocuments/marking criteriaexamples.pdf [Accessed 20 February 2021]

[4] https://bba.nus.edu.sg/wp-content/uploads/sites/37/2019/06/honors-dissertation-grading-scheme.pdf [Accessed 20 February 2021]

[5] www.york.ac.uk/media/healthsciences/documents/student-intranet/exams-assess/marking-criteria/MarkingCriteria_L7_diss.pdf [Accessed 20 February 2021]

References

200614195 (2014) *A critical discourse analysis of how women in top business and leadership roles were represented within* The Times *and* The New York Times *During March 2013*. BSc Hons Management dissertation: Leeds University Business School. Available at: http://resources.library.leeds.ac.uk/final-chapter/dissertations/lubs/3305example6.pdf

Allen, D. et al (in press) 'Paediatric early warning systems: development, implementation and evaluation of the PUMA programme: prospective mixed methods before and after study', *Health Services Delivery & Research*.

Amonashvili, N. (2011) *Education policy borrowing – Georgia: a case in point*. Masters' dissertation: Lund University Faculty of Social Sciences. Available at: https://lup.lub.lu.se/student-papers/search/publication/1974081 [Accessed 5 October 2021].

Atkinson, P. (2015) *For Ethnography*, London: SAGE.

Balch, A. and Balabanova, E. (2017) 'A deadly cocktail? The fusion of Europe and immigration in the UK press', *Critical Discourse Studies*, 14(3): 236–255.

Ball, M. (2010) 'Images, language and numbers in company reports: a study of documents that are occasioned by a legal requirement for financial disclosure', *Qualitative Research*, 11(2): 115–139.

Becker, H. (1986) *Writing for Social Scientists: How to Start and Finish Writing Your Thesis, Book or Article*, Chicago, IL: University of Chicago Press.

Bennett, L. and Kidd, J. (2017) 'Myths about media studies: the construction of media studies education in the British press', *Continuum*, 31(2): 163–176.

Blaggard, B.B. (2019) *Citizen Journalism as Conceptual Practice: Postcolonial Archives and Embodied Political Acts of New Media*, Frontiers of the Political: Doing International Politics, New York: Rowman & Littlefield.

Boynton, P.M. (2016) *The Research Companion: A Practical Guide for Those in the Social Sciences, Health and Development* (2nd edn), London: Routledge.

Braun, V. and Clarke, V. (2013) *Successful Qualitative Research: A Practical Guide for Beginners*, London: SAGE.

Braun, V. and Clarke, V. (2020) 'One size fits all? What counts as quality practice in (reflexive) thematic analysis?' *Qualitative Research in Psychology*, DOI: 10.1080/14780887.2020.1769238

Braun, V. and Clarke, V. (2021) 'Tips on writing a qualitative dissertation or thesis, from Braun & Clarke – Part 1', *Edpsy UK*. Available at: https://edpsy.org.uk/blog/2021/tips-on-writing-a-qualitative-dissertation-or-thesis-from-braun-clarke-part-1/

Brown, A. (2019) *Informed Is Best: How to Spot Fake News about Your Pregnancy, Birth and Baby*, London: Pinter and Martin.

Delamont, S., Atkinson, P. and Parry, O. (2004) *Supervising the Doctorate: A Guide to Success*, Milton Keynes: Open University Press.

Dickinson, J. (2020) 'Visualising the foreign and the domestic in diaspora diplomacy: images and the online politics of recognition in #givingtoindia', *Cambridge Review of International Affairs*, 33(5): 752–777, DOI: 10.1080/09557571.2020.1741512

Dickson-Swift, V., James, E.L., Kippen, S. and Liamputtong, P. (2009) 'Researching sensitive topics: qualitative research as emotion work', *Qualitative Research*, 9(1): 61–79.

Dowling, S. and Grant, A. (2021) 'An "incredible community" or "disgusting" and "weird"? Representations of breastmilk sharing in worldwide news media', *Maternal and Child Nutrition*, e13139, DOI: https://doi.org/10.1111/mcn.13139

franzke, a., Bechmann, A., Zimmer, M., Ess, C. and the Association of Internet Researchers (2020) 'Internet research: ethical guidelines 3.0', *Association of Internet Researchers* [online] 6 October 2019. Available at: https://aoir.org/eth ics/ [Accessed 21 December 2020].

Goffman, E. (1959) *The Presentation of Self in Everyday Life*, New York: Doubleday.

Grainger, R. and Minier, M. (2019) 'A paratextual analysis of nurturing opera audiences: transmedia practices, interactivity and historical interpretation in the Welsh National Opera's promotion of the "Tudors Trilogy"', *Participations: Journal of Audience and Reception Studies*, 16(1): 30–53.

Grant, A. (2016a) '#discrimination: the online response to a case of a breastfeeding mother being ejected from a UK retail premises', *Journal of Human Lactation*, 32(1): 141–151.

Grant, A. (2016b) ' "I ... don't want to see you flashing your bits around": exhibitionism, othering and good motherhood in perceptions of public breastfeeding', *Geoforum*, 71: 52–61.

Grant, A. (2018) 'Shock and offence online: the role of emotion in participant absent research', in T. Loughran and D. Mannay (eds) *Emotion and the Researcher: Sites, Subjectivities and Relationships*, Studies in Qualitative Methodology, Bingley: Emerald, pp 143–158.

Grant, A. (2019) *Doing Excellent Social Research with Documents: Practical Examples and Guidance for Qualitative Researchers*, Abingdon: Routledge.

Grant, A. (2021) 'Hidden Clues in Sources', in *Research Methods Primary Sources*. Marlborough: Adam Matthew Digital, DOI: 10.47594/RMPS_0037_HT

Grant, A. and Kara, H. (2021). 'Considering the autistic advantage in qualitative research: autistic researchers and qualitative data collection and analysis', *Contemporary Social Science*, DOI: 10.1080/21582041.2021.1998589.

Grant, A. and O'Mahoney, H. (2016) 'The portrayal of waterpipe (shisha, hookah, nargile) smoking on Twitter: a qualitative exploration', *Public Health*, 140: 128–135.

Hall, S. (1997) *Representation: Cultural Representations and Signifying Practices*, London: SAGE.

Harty, K.C. (1993) 'Animals and butts: Minnesota's media campaign against tobacco', *Tobacco Control*, 3: 271–274.

Houston, E. (2019) '"Risky" representation: the portrayal of women with mobility impairment in twenty-first-century advertising', *Disability & Society*, 34(5): 704–725.

Hoyle, L.P., Smith, E., Mahoney, C. and Kyle, R.G. (2018) 'Media depictions of "unacceptable" workplace violence towards nurses', *Policy, Politics, and Nursing Practice*, 19(3–4): 57–71.

Humphreys, L. (1970) *Tearoom Trade: Impersonal Sex in Public Places*, London: Duckworth.

Jolivette, A.J. (2015) *Research Justice: Methodologies for Change*, Bristol: Policy Press.

Judson, A. (2020) 'Scribes as editors: tracking changes in the Linear B Documents', *American Journal of Archaeology*, 124(4): 523–549.

Kara, H. (2017) *Research and Evaluation for Busy Students and Practitioners*, Bristol: Policy Press.

Kara, H. (2018a) *Research Ethics in the Real World: Euro-western and Indigenous Perspectives*, Bristol: Policy Press.

Kara, H. (2018b) *Little Quick Fix: Do Your Interviews*, London: SAGE.

Kara, H. (2020) 'Decolonising methods', *Helen Kara blog* [online] 29 July. Available at: https://helenkara.com/2020/07/29/decolonising-methods-a-reading-list/ [Accessed 27 February 2020].

Kersen, T.M. (2016) 'Insider/outsider: the unique nature of the sociological perspective and practice', *Journal of Applied Social Science*, 10(2): 104–112.

Kowalski, L. (2020) 'Hiding in plain sight: a mixed methods analysis of older adults who are reported missing in two Canadian cities'. Electronic Thesis and Dissertation Repository. 7460. https://ir.lib.uwo.ca/etd/7460

Latour, B. (2005) *Reassembling the Social: An Introduction to Actor Network Theory*, Oxford: Oxford University Press.

Lehner-Mear, R. (2020) 'Good mother, bad mother? Maternal identities and cyber-agency in the primary school homework debate', *Gender and Education*, DOI: 10.1080/09540253.2020.1763920

Levin, P. (2005) *Excellent Dissertations!* Milton Keynes: Open University Press.

Lipsky, M. (2011) *Street-level Bureaucracy: Dilemmas of the Individual in Public Services*, London: Russell Sage.

Loughran, T. and Mannay, D. (eds) (2018) *Emotion and the Researcher: Sites, Subjectivities and Relationships*, Studies in Qualitative Methodology, Bingley: Emerald.

Mann, C. and Stewart, F. (2000) *Internet Communication and Qualitative Research*, London: SAGE.

Mannay, D. (2016) *Visual Narrative and Creative Methods*, Abingdon: Routledge.

Mason, J. (2018) *Qualitative Researching*, London: SAGE.

McLean, J. (2020) *Changing Digital Geographies: Technologies, Environments and People*, London: Palgrave Macmillan.

Michie, S., van Stralen, M.M. and West, R. (2011) 'The behaviour change wheel: a new method for characterising and designing behaviour change interventions', *Implementation Science*, 6: 42.

Moher, D., Liberati, A., Tetzlaff, J., Altman, D.G. and The PRISMA Group (2009) 'Preferred reporting items for systematic reviews and meta-analyses: the PRISMA statement', *British Medical Journal*, 339: b2535.

Moore, N., Salter, A., Stanley, L. and Tamboukou, M. (2017) *The Archive Project: Archival Research in the Social Sciences*, Abingdon: Routledge.

Murray, O.M. (2018) *Doing feminist text-focused institutional ethnography in UK universities.* PhD Thesis: University of Edinburgh. Available at: https://era.ed.ac.uk/bitstream/handle/1842/35719/Murray2019.pdf?sequence=1&isAllowed=y

Mustafa, M.M. (2015) *Gendered space in the leisure landscapes of a modernising Islamic state.* PhD Thesis: Lincoln University, New Zealand. Available at: https://researcharchive.lincoln.ac.nz/handle/10182/6657

O'Hare, R. (2014) *A case study to evaluate the introduction of Objective Structured Clinical Examination (OSCE) within a school of pharmacy.* Doctor of Pharmacy Thesis: University of Derby. Available at: https://derby.openrepository.com/bitstream/handle/10545/337507/O%27Hare_Case_study_to_evaluate_introduction_of_Objective_Structured_Clinical_Examination_2014.pdf?sequence=1&isAllowed=y

Platt, J. (1981a) 'Evidence and proof in documentary research: 1 some specific problems of documentary research', *The Sociological Review*, 29(1): 31–52.

Platt, J. (1981b) 'Evidence and proof in documentary research: 2 some shared problems of documentary research', *The Sociological Review*, 29(1): 53–66.

Plummer, K. (2001) *Documents of Life 2: An Invitation to a Critical Humanism*, London: SAGE.

Prior, L. (2003) *Using Documents in Social Research*, London: SAGE.

Roberts, L.D. and Seaman, K. (2018) 'Students' experiences of undergraduate dissertation supervision', *Frontiers in Education* [online] 4 December. Available at: https://doi.org/10.3389/feduc.2018.00109 [Accessed 25 February 2021].

Russell-Pinson, L. and Harris, M.L. (2019) 'Anguish and anxiety, stress and strain: attending to writers' stress in the dissertation process', *Journal of Second Language Writing*, 43: 63–71.

Ryan, R.S. (2013) *The effect of online discussion forums on student learning and student perception of learning in a science course at the community college level.* PhD dissertation: University of Southern Mississippi. Available at: https://aquila.usm.edu/dissertations/207

Saldaña, J. (2015) *The Coding Manual for Qualitative Researchers*, London: SAGE.

Schreier, M. (2014) 'Qualitative content analysis', in U. Flick (ed) *The Sage Handbook of Qualitative Data Analysis*, London: SAGE, pp 170–183.

Scott, J. (1990) *A Matter of Record: Documentary Sources in Social Research*, London: John Wiley & Sons.

Skinner, J. (2015) *Ernestine Rose and the Harlem Public Library: theory testing using historical sources.* PhD Thesis: Florida State University. Available at: www.proquest.com/docview/1721391328/fulltextPDF/B86F1AC3A70D4251PQ/1?accountid=14680

Smith, D.E and Turner, R.M. (2014) *Incorporating Texts into Institutional Ethnographies*, Toronto: University of Toronto Press.

Terry, G., Hayfield, N., Clarke, V. and Braun, V. (2017) 'Thematic analysis', in C. Willig and W. Stainton Rogers (eds) *The Sage Handbook of Qualitative Research in Psychology*, London: SAGE, pp 17–37.

Thatcher, J. (2020) 'Interview with Dr Jenny Thatcher', *The Sociology Show Podcast* [online] 4 June. Available at: www.spreaker.com/user/thesociologyshow/dr-jenny-thatcher [Accessed 25 February 2021].

Todd, M., Bannister, P. and Clegg, S. (2004) 'Independent inquiry and the undergraduate dissertation: perceptions and experiences of final-year social science students', *Assessment & Evaluation in Higher Education*, 29(3): 335–355.

UCU (University College Union Anti-Casualisation Committee) (2020) 'Stamp out casual contracts', University College Union [online]. Available at: www.ucu.org.uk/stampout [Accessed 18 December 2020].

Waagen, S. (2016) *The passport: a perception of risk on mobility. A documentary analysis of the passport from a Norwegian view.* Master's dissertation: Sosiologisk institutt, Universitetet i Bergen. Available at: https://bora.uib.no/bora-xmlui/bitstream/handle/1956/12122/144341355.pdf?sequence=1&isAllowed=y

Ward, M. and Delamont, S. (2020) *Handbook of Qualitative Research in Education*, Cheltenham: Edward Elgar.

Whitehair, C. and Berdanier, C.G. (2018, June) *Capturing Narratives of Graduate Engineering Attrition through Online Forum Mining.* Paper presented at 2018 ASEE Annual Conference & Exposition, Salt Lake City, Utah. 10.18260/1-2—30176. Available at: https://peer.asee.org/capturing-narratives-of-graduate-engineering-attrition-through-online-forum-mining

Wiggins, S., Gordon-Finlayson, A., Becker, A. and Sullivan, C. (2016) 'Qualitative undergraduate project supervision in psychology: current practices and support needs of supervisors across North-East England and Scotland', *Qualitative Research in Psychology*, 13(1): 1–19.

Woods, R., Milton, D., Arnold, L. and Graby, S. (2018) 'Redefining Critical Autism Studies: a more inclusive interpretation', *Disability & Society*, 33(6): 974–979.

Wright, S. (2020) 'Creating liberal–internationalist world citizens: League of Nations Union junior branches in English secondary schools, 1919–1939', *Paedagogica Historica*, 56(3): 321–340. Available at: www.tandfonline.com/eprint/78ZgWkx2cR2Jt6849hXT/full

Zuberi, T. and Bonilla-Silva, E. (2008) *White Logic, White Methods: Racism and Methodology*, Plymouth: Rowman & Littlefield.

Index

References to figures, boxes, resources, sketch
notes and tables appear in **bold** type.